IMAGES
of America

STRAUB BREWERY

John E. Schlimm II

ARCADIA
PUBLISHING

Published by Arcadia Publishing
Charleston, South Carolina

Library of Congress Catalog Card Number: 2005925429

For all general information contact Arcadia Publishing at:
Telephone 843-853-2070
Fax 843-853-0044
E-mail sales@arcadiapublishing.com
For customer service and orders:
Toll-Free 1-888-313-2665

Visit us on the Internet at www.arcadiapublishing.com

CONTENTS

ACKNOWLEDGMENTS

This book would not have been possible without the help of several individuals: my parents, Jack and Barbara Schlimm; Mary Asti Anderson; Patty Straub Brock and the Straub Brewery Board of Directors; Dan and Cindy Straub; Thomas Straub; Joe McMackin; Carrie Whitaker; the employees of the Straub Brewery; Ray Beimel; Alice Beimel, Jenny Donachy, Barb Samick, and the Historical Society of St. Marys and Benzinger Township; John Skok; Bill and Mary Straub; Gloria Straub; Carleen Straub Koch; Denny Posteraro and family; the *Daily Press* of St. Marys; Kathy Jones, Linda Meabon, and the Zippo Manufacturing Company; Patty and Wray Burden; Steven K. Troha; and most especially the many grandparents, uncles, aunts, cousins, and friends who came before me and who *are* the history that is contained on the following pages. And, to anyone my mind and pen may have forgotten, please know that my heart never forgets. Also, to Kaia Motter and the entire Arcadia Publishing team, many thanks.

INTRODUCTION

From any western-facing window in my house, including the window next to my writing desk, I can see the Straub Brewery rising into the sky. The homestead of my great-grandparents, Francis and Rose Straub, lies to the east, as do those of my great-great-uncle Alfonse and aunt Laura Straub and my great-great-uncle Peter P. and aunt Mary Straub. To the south is great-great-uncle Tony and aunt Reggie Straub's homestead and great-great-uncle Joseph and aunt Elizabeth Straub's homestead. To the north is the former St. Marys Beverage Company, once also owned by the Straubs. I am literally surrounded by the history of my family and its brewery.

In compiling *Straub Brewery*, I was most inspired by my great-great-grandfather Peter Straub, who at the tender age of 19, left Germany in search of the American dream. He moved to St. Marys, Pennsylvania, where he met his wife, Sabina Sorg, and started working at my great-great-great-grandfather Francis Sorg's brewery in 1872. By 1878, Peter owned the brewery lock, stock, and you got it, beer barrel.

When I came across the following excerpt in the December 18, 1913, edition of the *Elk County Gazette*, I knew that I had at long last met my great-great-grandfather, a new role model: "Judged from every viewpoint, Mr. Straub was a man par excellent among men. His business principles were founded on the highest plane of honesty and fair dealing. As friend and neighbor, he was a tower of strength in times of stress and need. He never forgot the hospitality of the Vaterland, and his home was ever a home of welcome and good cheer to his many friends. Above all he was a Christian gentleman and in this respect his exemplary life will always remain an inspiration to all who came within the sphere of its influence. He no doubt, had his faults too, but they were hidden in the folds of his many manly virtues."

Likewise, I had the rare opportunity to reach into dusty brewery archives that had not been opened in 70, 80, 90 years and to shake hands with the mythical legends I have heard about all my life. I was also given the chance to reconnect with several cousins and others, including Mary Asti Anderson, Dan Straub, and Thomas Straub.

As an aspiring historian at best, I always worried that in finally sending this manuscript off to the publisher, I would forget to include something, but I then came to realize that history is a living, breathing, and ever-evolving entity that continually reveals new stories and truths, and to include everything would take an impossibly voluminous collection. I am satisfied that this is my contribution to the Straub Brewery history, my portrait of my family and its brewery at this moment in time. This is Peter's and our ongoing story.

My friend, Academy Award–nominated screenwriter Anna Hamilton Phelan, summarized my sentiments best when she wrote, "Straub Beer runs in our veins as well as blood."

Here's to our "eternal tap" on history!

—John E. Schlimm II
Straub Bear Run

There was an apple tree in Straub Bear Run that my grandmother always said grew from a special seed that was spit out by a lumberjack when the land was a lumbering camp. This tree, which was engulfed every spring in the most breathtaking pink and white blossoms, saw practically every generation of my family pass by. It shared our private tears and our gathered laughter, our quiet worries and our wildest dreams. It had a silent wisdom and rarity of the kind we are unlikely to ever see again. This tree—my American Bodhi Tree, which now belongs to the past, as do the pictures, memories, and words within this book—will forever inspire and strengthen me.

I dedicate this book and these memories to my parents, my family, and Straub drinkers everywhere—we are all one family—and, most especially, to our beloved Straub Bear Run and apple tree. You are, now and forever, my roots and my wings no matter where the path ahead leads. (Photograph by JES II.)

One

THE FOUNDING FAMILY

"We are a family and we are a tree; Our roots
go deep down in history; from my great-
great-granddaddy reaching up to me, we are
a green and growing family tree." —Song
performed by the younger Straub cousins at
the sixth Straub family reunion, July 1, 2000.

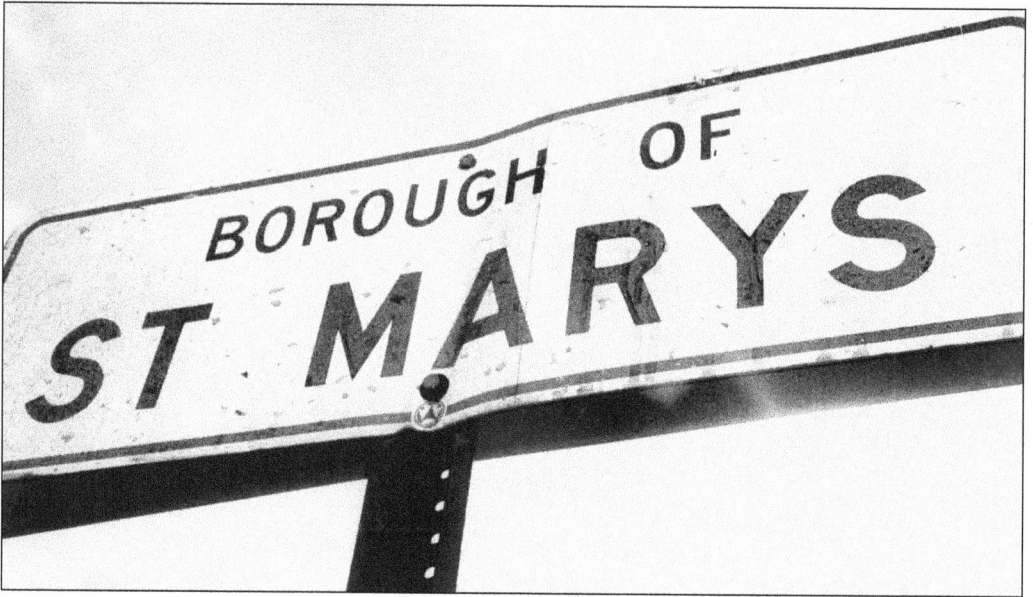

"Like apple pie and ice cream, cheese and crackers, ham and rye, Straub Beer and St. Marys seem to go together." —*History of the Straub Brewery*, 1980s. Hardly anyone can mention St. Marys, Pennsylvania, without identifying it with Straub beer. The Straub Brewery rests in the middle of the city of St. Marys, which was the borough of St. Marys until it merged with Benzinger Township. (Photograph by JES II.)

Peter Straub was born on June 28, 1850, in Felldorf, Wuerttemburg, Germany, to Anton and Anna M. Eger Straub. As a teenager, Peter was educated and worked as a cooper, which is a craftsman skilled in making and repairing wooden barrels and casks. He also became well versed in the allied trade of brewing. Peter honed his trade in Germany, France, and Switzerland. (Photograph by Ray Beimel, courtesy of Straub Brewery.)

At age 19 (in 1869), Peter Straub traveled to the United States and settled in Allegheny City, Pennsylvania, working at the Eberhardt and Ober Brewing Company. He next moved to Brookville and worked at the Christ and Allgeier Brewery. He again moved to Allegheny City and then to McKeesport and Centerville (later renamed Kersey). In 1872, Peter settled in St. Marys. Pictured are some of the tools he used. (Photograph by JES II, courtesy of Straub Brewery.)

WOOD from Original
BREWERY
1872

In St. Marys, Peter first worked at the Windfelder Brewery, which later became the Luhr Brewery, on Center Street. In the early 1870s, Peter was hired by Francis Sorg as brewmaster and manager for his brewery. The standard Straub Brewery founding date of 1872 reflects when Peter first moved to St. Marys and began brewing. He did not own the brewery until 1878. (Photograph by JES II, courtesy of Straub Brewery.)

Peter Straub began courting Francis Sorg's eldest daughter, Sabina, marrying her on November 23, 1875. A few years later, Peter and Sabina, along with their eldest son, Francis (one year old at the time), traveled back to Germany and then on to France, where they attended the Exposition Universelle in Paris. This portrait of Sabina hangs at the brewery. (Photograph by Ray Beimel, courtesy of Straub Brewery.)

Peter and Sabina had 10 children. Seen around 1904, the family members are, from left to right, as follows: (first row) Gerard Benedict (Gerry), Peter (Sr.), Mary Crescentia (Marian, later Mrs. Daniel Curran), Sabina holding Alfonse James (Ponce), and Peter Paul (Pete); (second row) Jacob Melchior (Fr. Gilbert), Joseph Anthony (Joe), Anna Angela (later Mrs. Frederick Luhr), Francis Xavier (Frank), and Anthony Albert (Tony). Another son, Peter Mathaeus (not pictured), died in 1892 at age two. (Courtesy of JES II.)

This early-1900s photograph shows eldest child Francis Straub, born on September 7, 1877, with his wife, Rose, and three of his children. The children are Gilbert (left), Esther (in back), and Rose. Francis served as a brewmaster at the brewery. (Courtesy of Bill and Mary Straub.)

Son Joseph, born on March 22, 1880, is pictured around 1900. He went on to be a brewmaster at the brewery. (Courtesy of JES II.)

This is son Anthony's First Communion portrait from the late 1800s. Anthony, born on July 17, 1882, went on to serve as the president of the brewery after his father. (Courtesy of Dan and Cindy Straub.)

This is eldest daughter Anna's First Communion picture from the late 1800s. Anna was born on October 28, 1884. (Courtesy of the Historical Society of St. Marys and Benzinger Township.)

This early-1900s photograph shows son Peter P. Straub, born on February 4, 1893. He went on to serve as the president of the brewery after Anthony. (Courtesy of the Historical Society of St. Marys and Benzinger Township.)

This portrait from the early 1900s shows son Gerard, born on September 20, 1896. He went on to become a lawyer and eventually serve as district attorney. (Courtesy of the Historical Society of St. Marys and Benzinger Township.)

Daughter Mary (also known as Marian) was born on November 16, 1899. She was the second daughter of Peter and Sabina. (Courtesy of the Historical Society of St. Marys and Benzinger Township.)

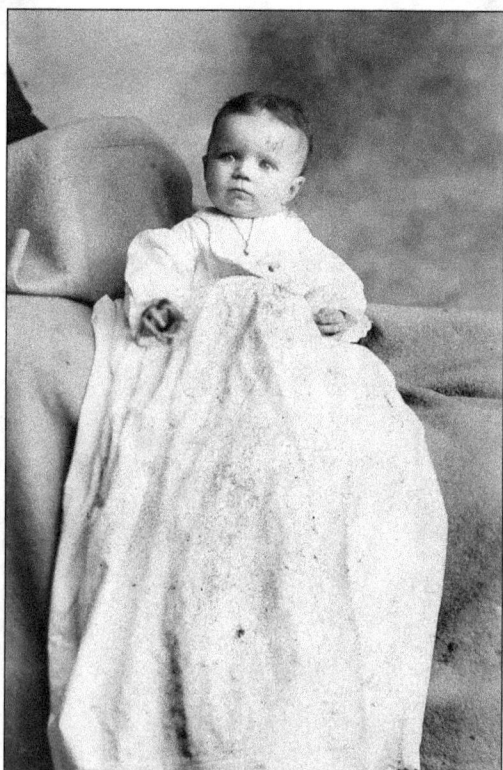

Son Alfonse was born on August 25, 1903. He went on to become a lawyer and provided legal counsel to the brewery. (Photograph by A. E. Warren, courtesy of Dan and Cindy Straub.)

Son Jacob, born on January 6, 1887, chose to enter the priesthood. Assuming Gilbert as his religious name, Fr. Gilbert Straub was ordained a Benedictine priest on June 24, 1913, at St. Vincent Archabbey. He performed his first mass at the St. Marys Church on July 6, 1913. (Courtesy of JES II.)

Peter and Sabina commemorated the event by giving their son a 14-karat gold chalice and paten decorated with amethysts and garnets. The chalice is now being used by Peter's great-grandson Fr. Paul Taylor, O.S.B., who was ordained at St. Vincent Archabbey on June 6, 1992. Peter's great-great-grandson, Herald Brock, was ordained Fr. Herald, C.F.R., at St. Patrick's Cathedral on May 14, 1994. (Photograph by Peter's great-granddaughter-in-law, Barbara Schlimm.)

Peter and Sabina's family and friends are pictured in the early 1900s. From left to right are the following: (first row) Peter P., Gerard, Anthony, Alfonse, Jake Sorg, and Francis; (second row) Fred Luhr, Fr. Philip Geiek, Amilia Carl, Fr. Gilbert, Peter, Anna, and John Carl; (third row) Al Custead, Crescentia Sorg Custead, Mary, Sabina, Florence Carl, and Maggie Sorg Carl. (Courtesy of the Historical Society of St. Marys and Benzinger Township.)

Hunting has long been a favorite pastime in Straub Country. This picture shows a few Straub family members and friends after a day of hunting, posing with the turkey they got. From left to right are the following: (first row) Carl Straub (Peter's grandson) and Alfonse; (second row) Gerard, unidentified, Ray Smith, Anthony, and Ferdie Schlimm (Peter's grandson-in-law). (Courtesy of the Historical Society of St. Marys and Benzinger Township.)

Peter and Sabina were very dedicated to their Catholic faith. This stained-glass window, depicting Jesus handing the keys of the church to St. Peter, was donated by Peter and Sabina to the Sacred Heart Church in St. Marys in 1908–1909. An inscription in the lower right-hand corner reads, "Gift of Peter Straub." (Photograph by JES II.)

This stained-glass window, also depicting Jesus handing the keys of the church to St. Peter, was donated by Peter and Sabina to the St. Marys Church during the second installation of the church's stained-glass windows in 1910. The German inscription at the bottom reads, "Geschenk Von Peter Straub and Familie," which translates to "Gift of Peter Straub and Family." (Photograph by JES II.)

Following Peter's death, Anthony and Peter P. served as brewery president, respectively. Francis served as brewmaster. Alfonse and Gerard both became lawyers, the first serving as counsel for the brewery and the latter serving as district attorney for many years. This early-1900s photograph shows, from left to right, Jacob (Fr. Gilbert), Francis, and Peter P. with the brewery and wooden barrels in the background. (Courtesy of JES II.)

Following Peter P.'s death, Peter's grandson Jim Straub became brewery president. Jim was followed by Peter's grandson Herbert Straub, and Peter's great-grandson, Dan Straub, who currently holds the position. Shown from left to right are Herbert, Gilbert, and Jim. This photograph later inspired a caricature rendering of the three men that was used on the back of a T-shirt. (Courtesy of Straub Brewery.)

Peter and Sabina also owned the Straub Dairy Farm on Windfall Road, which produced milk, chocolate milk, butter, and cream. The farm was initially supervised and run by Peter P. and later by Mr. and Mrs. Art Anderson, who resided there. The location is now the site of a corporate plant. This is not the original Straub barn but one built later on the same site. (Photograph by JES II.)

Shown is a milk bottle from the Straub Dairy Farm. (Photograph by JES II, courtesy of JES II.)

Sabina was known to generously dispense Straub milk and other products from her home in town to individuals who could not afford to buy them. This is a portrait of Sabina on the occasion of her daughter Mary's wedding to Daniel Curran on November 24, 1930. (Courtesy of the Historical Society of St. Marys and Benzinger Township.)

STRAUB'S STORE
"QUALITY FARM SERVICE"
HARDWARE -- HEATING -- APPLIANCES
MACHINERY
MARATHON, WISCONSIN 54448.   TELEPHONE 6/ 443 2653

The Brewery Straubs
St. Marys Penn. 15857.

Dear Fellow Straubs,

    Last week my brother, Tony Straub, made a social call at your Brewery, and brought back the October Issue of "Roaming" with the wonderful writeup of Beer and and Straub Brewery at St. Marys.

    Since my retirement from the above mentioned Store business, my hobby has been History and Genealogy. It so happened that I had part of your family tree in my files since 1956 - possibly from Father Gilbert Straub.

    I am enclosing copies of summaries of your and my family trees for someone in your relationship to keep and expand. It is very interesting that both of our ancestors came from Oberant Horb, Wuettemberg, Germany. It sure would be interesting to find the connection. If it is found by one of your relatives they should let me know, and if found here, I will. Incidently, the two pages on your family are all I have. So let someone bring it down to your and the younger generations and send me a listing.

    It sure was great to learn about you and your brewery.
    Hoping to hear from one of you again, I am Sincerely
                    yours   Al Straub
                               Alfred   Straub
                               5th & Walnut Sts.
                               Marathon
Ps. I went out of business   Wis.   54448
  in 1960 after 23 years.
  Had to get bigger or get out.

This is a note from Alfred Straub of Marathon, Wisconsin, to "the Brewery Straubs." Although not related, he kindly sent information regarding the origin of the Straub name. A family history that Alfred believed might have been compiled by Fr. Gilbert Straub, states, "The name Straub seems to be derived from the City of Straubing in Southern Germany, since all branches of Straubs originate within 200 miles of this city." (Courtesy of Straub Brewery.)

The family history goes on to say, "In the year 530 B.C. a certain Strubo was an outstanding leader in this community [what would become Straubing, Germany] along the Danube River and the settlement was named Strubonium. Before 1000 A.D. this name was varied to Straubingen. In the 12th Century A.D. it was shortened to Straubing which this City of 41,000 inhabitants is still called in 1955." (Courtesy of Straub Brewery.)

The Straub Brewery remains one of the only small breweries in the country to still be owned and operated by its founding family. Several Straub family members work at the brewery along with other local residents, such as Peter's great-great-granddaughter Mary Asti Anderson, who works in the brewery office. (Photograph by JES II.)

"The Straub crest or shield had the image of a peacock (Straus-Vogel), and a bunch of grapes (traube). It was to mean 'Proud love of farming' (Liebe sur Landswiertshaft)." —From a history sent to the Straub Brewery by Alfred Straub of Marathon, Wisconsin. This is the Straub family crest from the fourth Straub family reunion T-shirt, July 3, 1993. (Photograph by JES II, courtesy of JES II.)

Straub family reunions are held every five years at Straub Bear Run. For the 2000 Straub family reunion and in celebration of the new millennium, Peter's great-great-grandson John E. Schlimm II spearheaded an effort to bury a time capsule. It contains a journal in which family members wrote reflections and messages to the future generations and other relics contributed by the brewery and family. (Photograph by Allen Herr.)

On a Fourth of July during the 1960s, Peter's grandson, Frank Straub, took his restless grandchildren for a walk in Straub Bear Run. The walk grew in size over the years and turned into the annual Straub family Fourth of July parade that starts promptly at 4:00 p.m. with the ringing of the bell at Frank's Orchard Lodge camp. Frank became the family's very own Uncle Sam. (Photograph by Allen Herr.)

Gilbert Straub and his wife, Laura, served as the family's very own George and Martha Washington during several parades, including this one in the early 1980s. (Photograph by Barbara Schlimm.)

The younger Straubs dress up and decorate their bikes and pets for the parade. This is Peter Straub's great-great-great-grandson, Tony Chiappelli, after riding in the parade in the late 1990s. (Photograph by JES II.)

Peter's great-great-great-grandsons, Ian and Nathan Straub, wave their flags during part of the parade in the late 1990s. (Photograph by JES II.)

Peter's granddaughter Irene "Blondie" Straub Taylor leads the singing of religious and patriotic songs as the parade in the late 1990s progresses from Orchard Lodge, to the Flat Camp, to the Blessed Mother's Grotto, where deceased family and friends are remembered, and finally to Peter P.'s "Uncle Pete's Camp." The parade is always led by Peter's great-grandson Peter Bosnik, who carries the large flag. (Photograph by JES II.)

Even the elder Straubs joined in the parade by riding on a flatbed pulled by a tractor. This photograph was taken on July 4, 1976, the 200th birthday of the United States. Seen with various younger Straubs are, from left to right, Peter's daughter-in-law Minnie Straub, Peter's granddaughter Esther Straub Schlimm, Peter's daughter-in-law Reggie Straub, and Peter's granddaughter-in-law Peg Straub (also known as "Mrs. Sam," as she was married to "Uncle Sam"). (Photograph by Allen Herr.)

Peter's great-great-grandson Rick Straub has often played taps during the final phase of the parade, including this one during the late 1990s. Rick also worked at the brewery at one time. (Photograph by JES II.)

Peter's grandson Vic Straub brings the parade to a close around the flagpole at Uncle Pete's Camp with a reflective speech about America. Peter Bosnik is seen holding the flag to the left as the family gathers around the larger flagpole. (Photograph by JES II.)

Anthony's wife, Regina (known as "Aunt Reggie" to family and friends alike), turned 100 on September 21, 1987, becoming the only family member to live to that age. She went on to live four more years to secure her record. (Courtesy of JES II.)

You are cordially invited

to attend the celebration of

Regina S. Straub's

100th Birthday

Sunday, the twentieth of September

nineteen hundred and eighty-seven

Mass at four p.m.

St. Marys Church

with dinner immediately following

at the St. Marys Grade School

No gifts please
Regrets only
M. Smith 834-3706
P. Brock 834-6976

This is John E. Schlimm II and Aunt Reggie on New Year's Eve 1977. John crowned Aunt Reggie the queen of New Year's, and she dutifully returned the favor by crowning him the king, salutations that they would fondly and forever thereafter use for one another. (Photograph by Barbara Schlimm.)

The new generation of Straubs will go to any height—or depth—to celebrate their heritage. Brewery president Dan Straub and a drinking buddy enjoy a Straub's under the sea. Surely, the bottom of the ocean never tasted so good! (Photograph by Denny Posteraro.)

Two

OUTSIDE LOOKING IN

"Up to 1840, 'British' type of beer dominated the American scene, but enough is enough, the Germans said and took it upon themselves to educate the Americans on real beer, the lager variety, which is today America's basic taste bud wetter. And this in turn brings us to the story of the Straub Brewery, one of the oldest manufacturing concerns in St. Marys." —Roswitha Cheatle, *Roaming*, October 1975.

Brewing in St. Marys dates to just after its founding in 1842. The first St. Marys brewery was built in 1845 by Michael Hantz. Others included Edward Babel's Babylon Brewery (1870), which was operated by the early Benedictine Fathers, and Joseph Windfelder's brewery (1851), where Peter first worked in town. This early photograph shows the Windfelder Brewery. (Courtesy of the Historical Society of St. Marys and Benzinger Township.)

Two other breweries were Burgess and Wesnitzer's Mountain Brewery (1880) and Col. William Kaul's St. Marys Beverage Company (1900). This portrait of four delivery teams at the St. Marys Beverage Company was taken between 1900 and 1920. (Courtesy of the Historical Society of St. Marys and Benzinger Township.)

It was Mexican War and Civil War veteran Capt. Charles C. Volk's brewery (1855) that would one day become the community's only brewery. This is Volk's eatery and saloon, which was originally on Erie Avenue until it burned down and he moved the operation to what is now Sorg Street. (Drawing by Charles Schaut, courtesy of the Historical Society of St. Marys and Benzinger Township.)

Taken around 1868, this is the earliest known picture of St. Marys. On the hill to the left is Volk's brewery on what is the current site of the Straub Brewery. (Courtesy of the Historical Society of St. Marys and Benzinger Township.)

On December 2, 1869, Francis Sorg purchased Capt. Charles C. Volk's brewery. On June 7, 1873, Francis sold half of his interest to Bernhard Wesnitzer, forming a brewery called Sorg and Wesnitzer on September 1, 1873. On September 2, 1876, Peter purchased Francis's share of Sorg and Wesnitzer. In 1878, Peter bought out Bernhard Wesnitzer's interest. Peter's brewery, which was called the Benzinger Spring Brewery, is shown around 1895. Peter is standing to the left of the barrel. Francis is on the wagon to the left, and Peter P. is on the bike. Brewery cooper John Kraus is in the cask. Joseph and Jake Sorg are standing beside the cask. Anthony is on the wagon to the right. (Courtesy of JES II.)

This portrait of the brewery wash house dates from the mid-1900s and is one of the few existing photographs from that period. (Courtesy of the Historical Society of St. Marys and Benzinger Township.)

In 1916, the old Peter Straub Sons brew house was torn down and replaced by the three-story brick building that forms the foundation of today's brewery. This picture is from the first half of the 1900s. (Courtesy of the Historical Society of St. Marys and Benzinger Township.)

THE BOROUGH OF ST. MARYS

BUILDING PERMIT   No. 465

In pursuance of a certain Application For Building Permit dated ..... June 26 ...., 19 40
and of action thereon taken by the Borough Council, but without assuming any liability on the part of the Borough of
St. Marys, a Permit is hereby granted to ... Straub Brothers ...., the applicant named in the
said Application, to ERECT REMODEL ENLARGE RECONSTRUCT MOVE a building to be used as a
... Bottling plant .... upon land of the applicant situate on the ...... East ....
side of ..... South .... Street, at No. .... (OR) .... feet
Rear of No 303
from .... in accordance
with the statements, specifications and plans contained in the said Application or filed therewith, upon and subject to
the following conditions, viz:

1. That the same shall be done in every respect in conformity with all laws of the Commonwealth of
Pennsylvania and all Ordinances and regulations of the Borough of St. Marys and the rules and regulations
of the Department of Health of the Commonwealth of Pennsylvania and of the Board of Health of the Borough
of St. Marys:
2. That the proposed construction shall be begun within six (6) months after the date hereof and shall
be completed within eighteen (18) months after the date hereof, otherwise this Permit shall be and become
null and void:
3. That the Building Permit card which is issued with this Permit shall be conspicuously displayed, in
plain view from the public highway, upon the principal frontage of the premises upon which construction under
this Permit is being carried on, at all times after beginning such construction until the same shall have been
completed.
and also upon and subject to the following special conditions, viz: .... None ....
....

....
and the acceptance of this Permit by the said applicant, and the payment of the required fee therefor, or the beginning of the proposed construction under this Permit, shall be deemed and taken to be an acceptance upon the part of
the applicant of all of the said conditions hereinabove contained and a covenant upon his part at all times to fully
comply in every respect with the said conditions.

Issued ...... June 26 ...., 19 40.   ....
                                                Borough Secretary of
                                                The Borough of St. Marys.

(SEE NOTICE ON REVERSE)

In late November 1940, a bottling plant was added to the Peter Straub Sons Brewery (also called the Straub Brothers Brewery), ringing in the era of bottled beer in addition to the draught beer that had been produced since the beginning. This is the building permit for the new bottling plant. (Courtesy of Straub Brewery.)

This is the front of the brewery in the 1960s. In his book *Pennsylvania Breweries*, Lew Bryson writes of the brewery, "It is, by Straub family reckoning, the highest brewery in the East, sitting at an elevation between 1,900 and 2,000 feet above sea level. This puts the brewery just below the Eastern Continental Divide, which means, as Dan Straub laughingly claims, 'We get to use the water first!'" (Courtesy of JES II.)

In 1920, the Straub Brothers Brewery purchased one half of the St. Marys Beverage Company, also called the St. Marys Brewery, where St. Marys Beer was produced. On July 19, 1940, the Straub Brothers Brewery purchased the remaining common stock and outstanding bonds of the St. Marys Beverage Company from Col. William Kaul. This photograph of the St. Marys Beverage Company was taken sometime after 1910 but before Prohibition. (Courtesy of Ray Beimel.)

The St. Marys Beverage Company stationery (under Straub control) advertised that they were "Brewers and Bottlers of High Grade Lager Beer." This is a stock certificate from the St. Marys Beverage Company. (Courtesy of Straub Brewery.)

From December 31, 1940, to March 1, 1950, portions of the St. Marys Beverage Company were leased to the Stackpole Carbon Company. This c. 1933 picture shows the icehouse to the far right and other buildings behind the St. Marys Beverage Company. (Courtesy of JES II.)

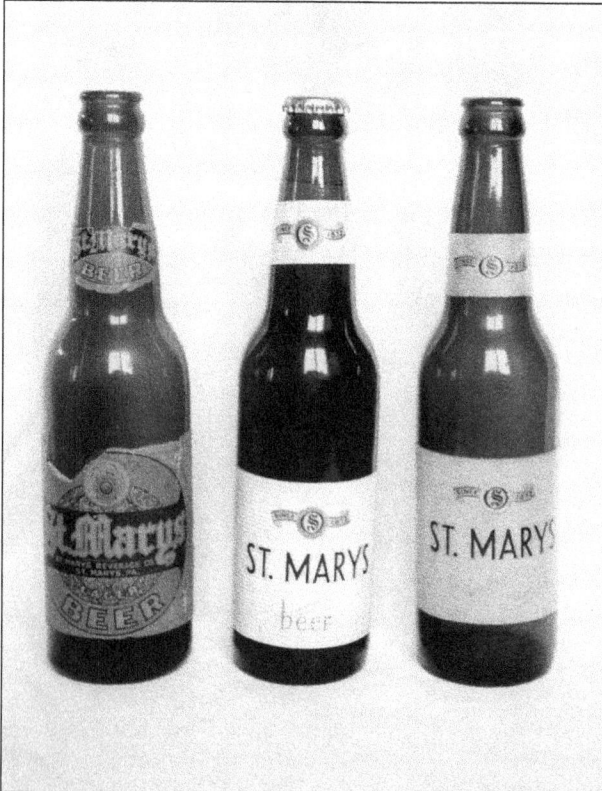

These vintage beer bottles produced by both the Straub Brewery and St. Marys Beverage Company demonstrate both companies' affection for their hometown roots. (Photograph by JES II, courtesy of Straub Brewery.)

During the late 1950s, the Straub Brothers Brewery sold the St. Marys Beverage Company property to the Pure Carbon Company, which had previously also leased the property. This is an early-1900s wintry scene of the wooden barrels and delivery wagons at the St. Marys Beverage Company. (Courtesy of the Historical Society of St. Marys and Benzinger Township.)

The Straub Brewery has been very fortunate to face only a few catastrophes. One of the most notable events occurred on July 11, 1971, when the old brewery barn-turned-warehouse burned, during which the ceiling gave way and 1,500 half-barrel aluminum kegs came rolling out. The porch post visible in the right-hand corner is part of the Peter and Sabina homestead, in which Peter P.'s family also lived at one time. (Courtesy of the Daily Press.)

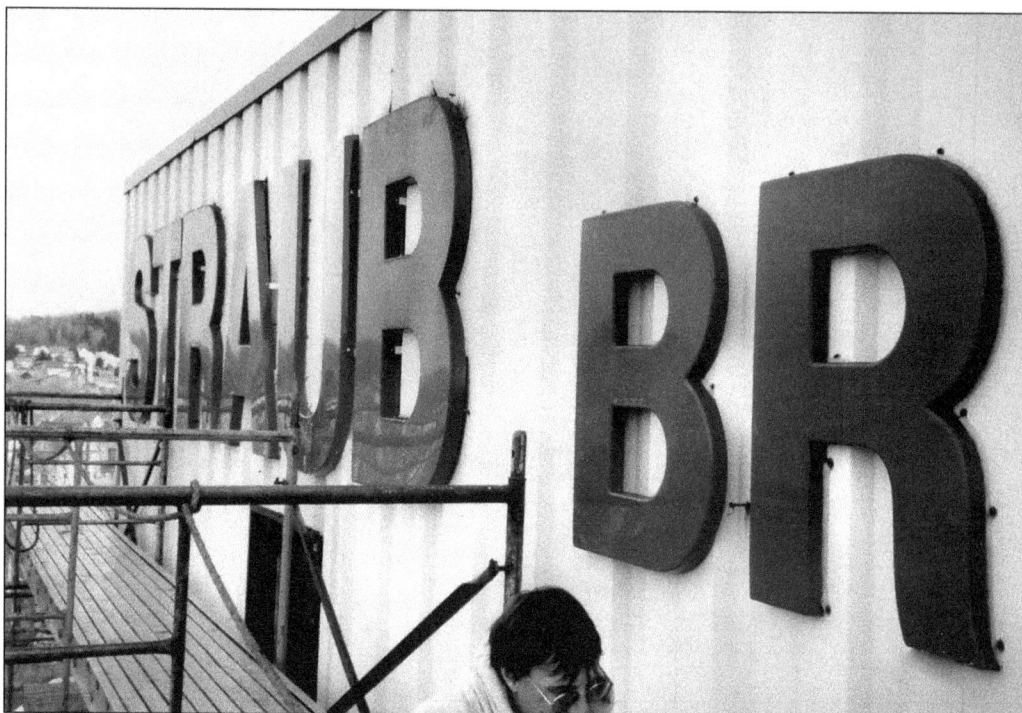

A minor catastrophe occurred in 2002 when the letter *U* in the large red "Straub Brewery" written across the front of the brewery fell off. Peter's great-grandson and current brewmaster and vice president Thomas Straub recalls having to phone the company that made the letters and say, "I would like to buy a vowel!" (Photograph by Thomas Straub.)

This is the brewery as it is today, located at 303 Sorg Street. It is the oldest manufacturing plant in operation in Elk County. Customers can pull right up to the front door and have beer loaded into their car and then drive around to the side to either go for a tour or browse in the gift shop. (Photograph by JES II.)

During the late 1800s and early 1900s, Straub beer was delivered by horse and wagon to an ever-growing roster of customers. In this *c.* 1906 photograph, Charles Dippold delivers beer on Brussells Street. (Courtesy of JES II.)

This is a portrait of Charles Dippold with his beer-delivery wagon in 1906. (Courtesy of the Historical Society of St. Marys and Benzinger Township.)

As advances were made in delivery transportation and the demand for Straub beer increased, the horses and wagons at the brewery were replaced by more expedient means of transportation, including this 1996 Chevy Cheyenne delivery truck, which is still being used. (Photograph by Thomas Straub.)

This larger truck, as well as a semitruck, also ensures that Straub beer gets to its destinations throughout Pennsylvania and Ohio. Here, the brewery truck makes a delivery at the local CYMA. (Courtesy of Straub Brewery.)

From the days of horse-and-wagon deliveries to truck drop-offs, the personal touch has never been lost. The Straub lettering design on the back of this truck is a welcome sign to many a local resident as it holds in the brewed goods. The metal design was handcrafted by the maintenance team at the brewery in 2002. (Photograph by Thomas Straub.)

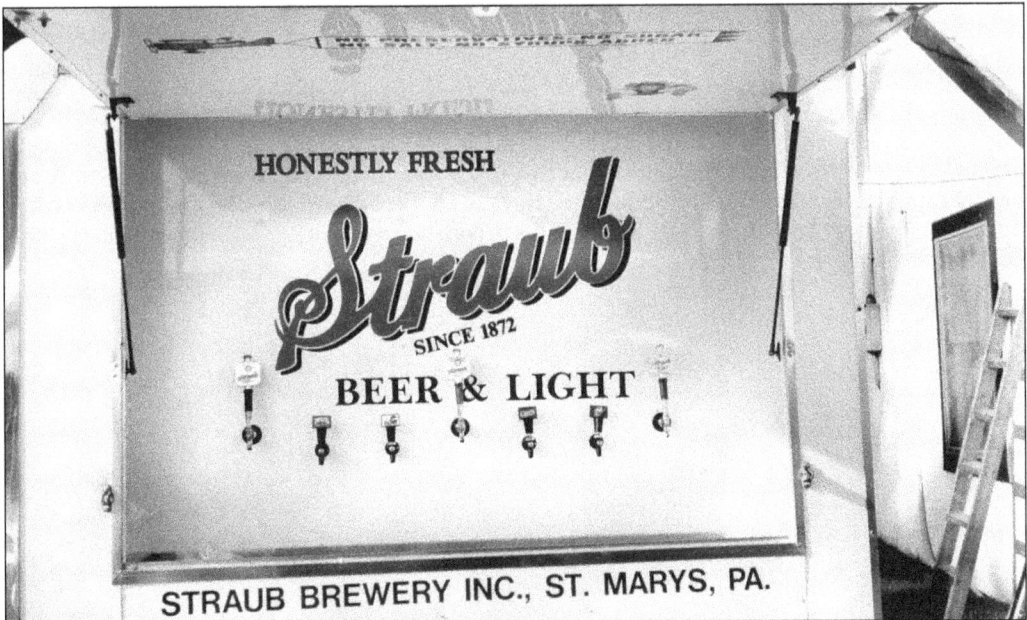

For those Straub beer parties, the brewery also has a small truck with taps right in back. On this day, the truck was keeping a Straub family reunion well stocked with Straub's. (Photograph by Barbara Schlimm.)

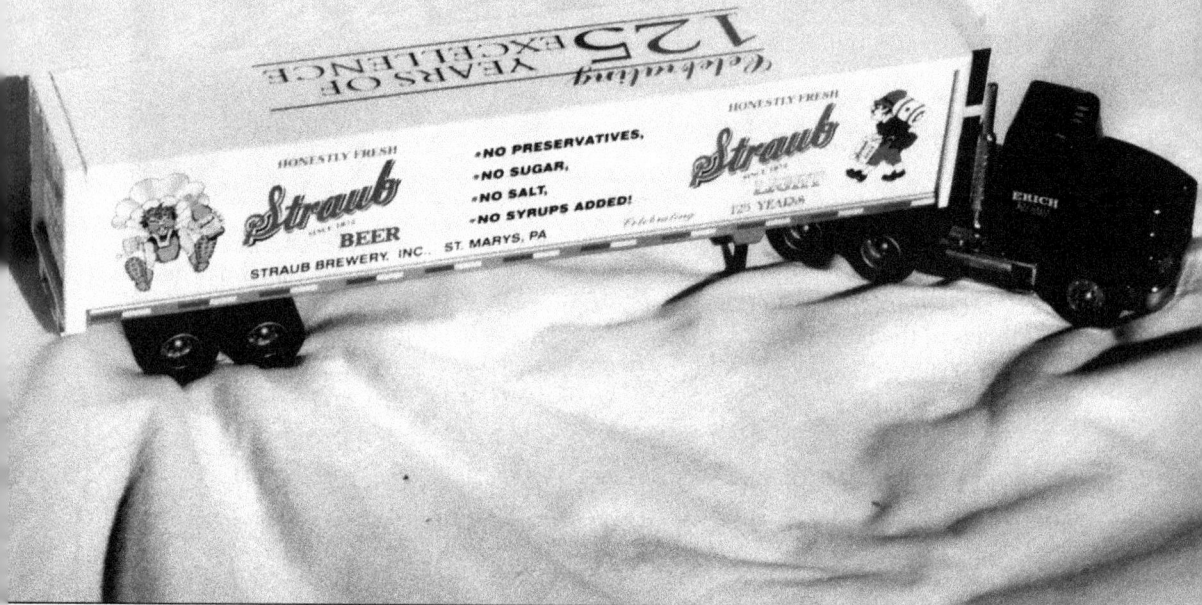

During its 125th anniversary, the brewery commissioned and sold this miniature version of its large Erich Rental delivery truck. Brewery trucks have always been headline grabbers in their own right, as is evident in a *Daily Press* article from May 2, 1938: "When a man bites a dog that's news. When beer truck hits beer truck that is also news. This news happened this morning around 10:30 when a St. Marys brewery beer truck . . . collided with a Straub brewery truck. . . . No great damage done. Beer market remains steady." (Photograph by JES II.)

Three

WHERE THE GOLD FLOWS

"The Editor who assigns himself to write a profile of the Straub Brewery is in for a pleasurably educational experience—one that is, among other things, soothing to the psyche and respectful to the taste buds."
—*Brewers Digest*, July 1980.

It all starts in the brewmaster's office. In a world of large, national breweries, the Straub Brewery comfortably remains a small regional macrobrewery and one of only a few that is still owned and operated by its founding family. The brewery is considered a craft brewery, where much of the brewing is orchestrated by human hands and not by elaborate machinery in mass production. (Photograph by JES II.)

Early on, Peter introduced his sons to the world of brewing. Here, Peter proudly poses with Francis (left) and Joseph (right). (Courtesy of JES II.)

Following Peter's death on December 17, 1913, his sons assumed control of the brewery, renaming it the Peter Straub Sons Brewery. During this time, the brewery produced Straub beer as well as other beer, such as the pilsner-style Straub Fine Beer and Straub Bock Beer. This Peter Straub Sons Brewery ledger displays various business transactions from 1913 to 1923. (Photograph by JES II, courtesy of Peter's great granddaughter Carleen Straub Koch.)

This stock certificate, dated January 26, 1923, was issued to Francis for his share of the Peter Straub Sons Brewery. Similar certificates were issued to the other siblings. The Peter Straub Sons stationery at the time referred to the company as "Brewers of High Grade Beers." During Prohibition, which lasted from January 29, 1920, until December 5, 1933, the brewery produced nonalcoholic near-beer. (Courtesy of Straub Brewery.)

Form WAP-3—1M—6-33

GENERAL No. 361

SERIAL No. G-128

COMMONWEALTH OF PENNSYLVANIA
ALCOHOL PERMIT BOARD
PERMIT

Harrisburg, Pennsylvania,

July 25, 1933

To   Straub Brewery

St. Marys, Pennsylvania

Application and bond having been duly presented and approved, you are hereby authorized to operate a - - - - BREWER OR MANUFACTURER OF CEREAL BEVERAGES

Located at   Rear 303 Sorg Street, St. Marys, Pennsylvania

This permit authorizes the permittee to manufacture, produce, distill, develop, use in the process of manufacture, redistill, recover, reuse, store, sell at wholesale, and remove alcohol or alcoholic liquid produced in the process of operating a brewery or cereal beverage plant, all in full accordance with the laws and regulations of the United States and the Commonwealth of Pennsylvania applying to breweries and manufacturers of cereal beverages.

The business hereby permitted shall at all times be subject to inspection by the members of the Board and the persons duly authorized and designated by the Board shall have the right, without fee or hindrance, to enter any place which is subject to inspection hereunder, or any place, where records subject to inspection under the Act of February 19, 1926, P. L. 16, are kept for the purpose of making such inspection.

Violation of any provision of law or regulation of the United States or the Commonwealth of Pennsylvania relating to the business authorized by this permit, shall be grounds for citation for revocation hereof.

This permit is not transferable or assignable.

This permit expires December 31, 19 33, unless sooner revoked or cancelled.

COMMONWEALTH OF PENNSYLVANIA
ALCOHOL PERMIT BOARD

By _____
Chairman

_____
Member

_____
Member

Penal Provision: Sec. 20, Act of February 19, 1926, P. L. 16.

Section 20. Any person or persons, who knowingly violate any of the provisions of this act, or any person who shall violate any of the conditions of any permit, or who shall falsify any record or report required by this act to be kept, or who shall violate any rule or regulation of the board, or who shall interfere with, hinder or obstruct any inspection authorized by this act, or prevent any member of the board, or any person duly authorized and designated by the board, from entering any place which such member of the board, or such person, is authorized by this act to enter for the purpose of making an inspection, or who shall violate any other provision of this act, shall be guilty of a misdemeanor, and, upon conviction thereof, shall be sentenced to pay a fine of not less than one hundred dollars ($100.00) nor more than five thousand dollars ($5,000.00), or undergo imprisonment of not more than three (3) years, or both, at the discretion of the court.

This is the 1933 alcohol permit given to the brewery by the Commonwealth of Pennsylvania following Prohibition. In 1947, the brewery was incorporated, becoming the Straub Brewery Inc. Before and after this date, the brewery would also be referred to as the Straub Brothers Brewery in some official and legal documentation. (Courtesy of Straub Brewery.)

The recipe for Straub beer is little changed, other than advances in technology and transportation, since the days when Peter and his sons were at the helm. For example, even today, the brewery may be the only one left in the country that still uses a Lampson carbonating stone for natural carbonation. Here, the truck is delivering the malted barley and pumping it into the metal silo. (Photograph by Thomas Straub.)

The malted barley goes into the malt mill, where it is cracked and processed into a meal called grist. This is the old malt mill from the latter half of the 1900s. (Photograph by Thomas Straub.)

The Straub beer recipe begins at 4:00 a.m. with its main ingredient, mountain-fed spring and stream water from the Laurel Run Reservoir. Some 5,000 gallons of water are used during one day of brewing. The water is combined with corn flakes and crushed malted barley and mixed in the mash-lauter tub or mash tub. Here, the brewery's old mash tub (c. 1940s) is being removed. (Photograph by Thomas Straub.)

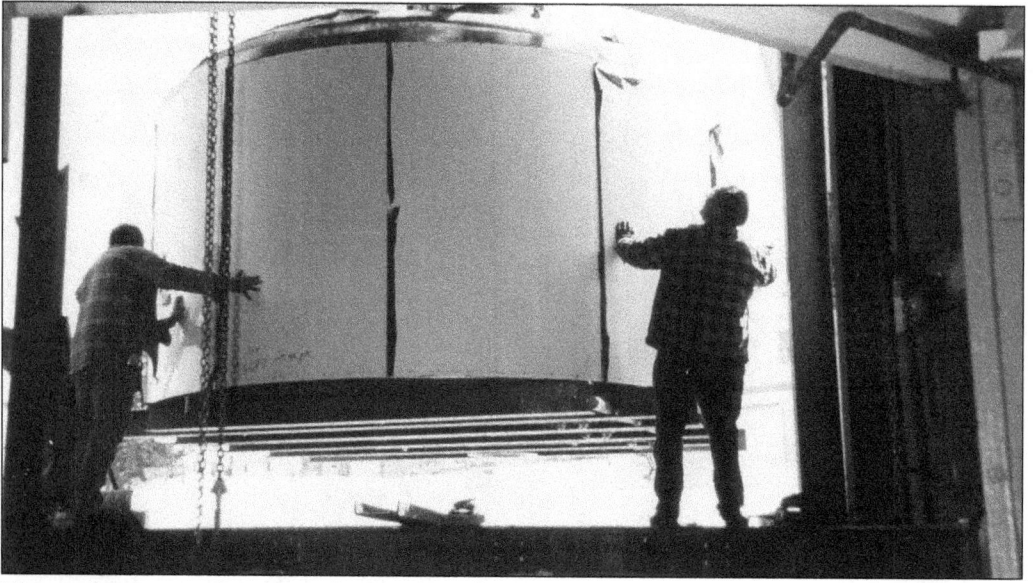

This is the new, updated stainless steel mash tub arriving via crane around 1995. During the 1990s, the brewery entered the decade of stainless steel, replacing many pieces of equipment, such as the famous Copper Kettle, with a new stainless steel kettle, storage tank, labeler, filler, and double-deck pasteurizer. (Photograph by Thomas Straub.)

The starch from the grains is converted into fermentable sugar by the natural enzymes contained in the malted barley. The mixing process lasts for two and a half hours at temperatures ranging from 104 to 170 degrees, producing a sweet golden syrup called wort. The old wort tank (c. 1982) was recycled into a water-recovery tank. Here, the new wort tank is in place and ready for brewing. (Photograph by Thomas Straub.)

The wort is slowly drawn through a copper vessel called a grant, where it is visually inspected for clarity and color. This is the antique grant that has been used to make Straub beer since the first half of the 1900s. After 1995, this grant was shortened and refitted with six draw pipes and 12 draw points. The original, shown above, had eight draw pipes and eight draw points. (Photograph by Ray Beimel.)

Next, hops extract is added as the wort is transferred through the grant to the brew kettle, where it is boiled for two hours. A large copper kettle was used in the brewing process at the brewery for most the 1900s. This antiquated kettle was one of most popular tourist attractions and most photographed sites next to the Eternal Tap on the brewery tour. (Photograph by Ray Beimel.)

The famed Copper Kettle was created in 1883 and won the grand prize at the Columbian World's Exposition during that year. It was purchased by the St. Marys Beverage Company in 1901 and then by the Straub Brewery in the 1940s. The kettle was decommissioned and scrapped in 1995. However, the brewery did salvage the door and a few other pieces for archival and nostalgic purposes. (Photograph by Thomas Straub.)

In 1995, the new stainless steel kettle arrived. It was delivered in pieces and field-erected on-site. Here, the new percolator, which ensures a rolling boil so as to superheat the bottom of the kettle and send the heat upward throughout the kettle during the brewing process, is being put in place. (Photograph by Thomas Straub.)

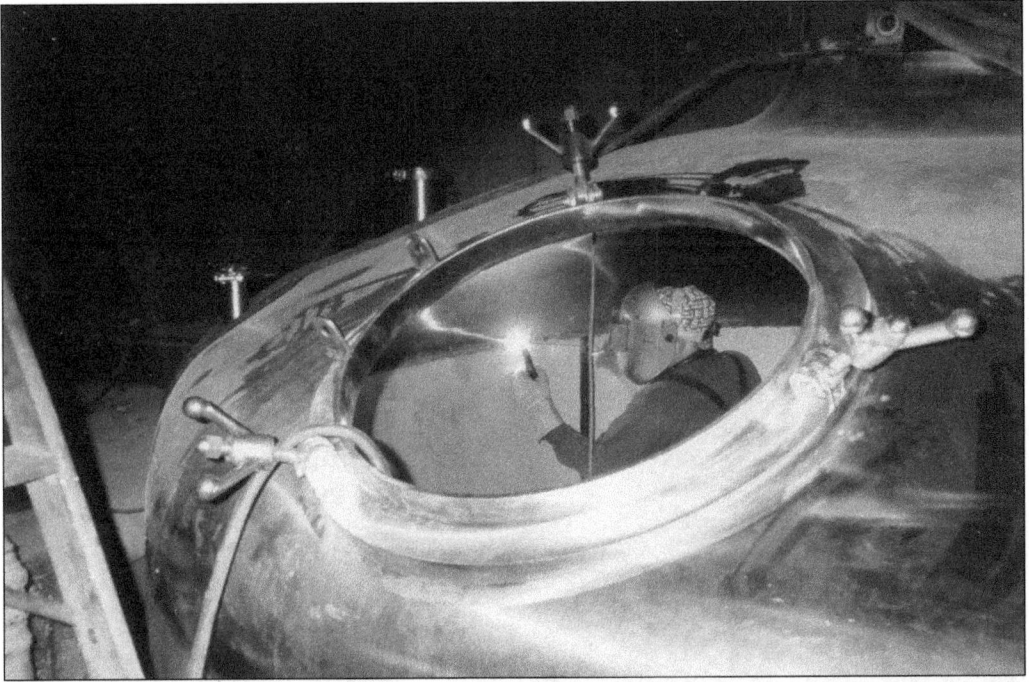

In this photograph, a craftsman attaches the new head of the kettle to the new side wall. (Photograph by Thomas Straub.)

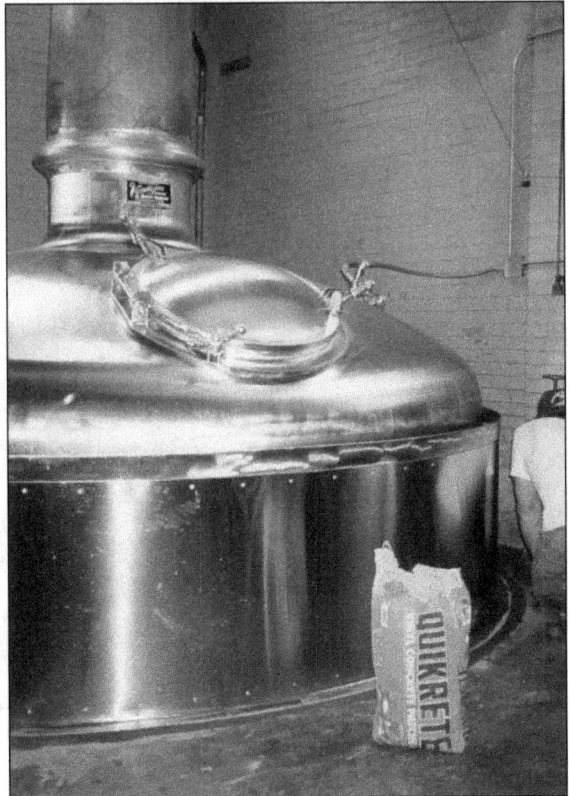

Although the new kettle helped to ring in the brewery's era of stainless steel, as seen here, the original copper vapor stack on top is still in use today, linking the old with the new. (Photograph by Thomas Straub.)

The heated mixture is held in a separate vessel for a short time before being cooled to approximately 54 degrees as it passes through an enclosed wort-cooling system at a rate of one barrel per minute and then proceeds to the fermenting tanks. In this early-1970s photograph, former brewmaster Jim Haberberger inspects the vintage open wort cooler that was used until 1982. (Photograph by Ray Beimel.)

The fermenting process begins with the addition of liquid yeast to the unfermented beer. These are the vintage carbon steel, glass-lined fermenting tanks that were used for the better part of the 1900s. (Photograph by Thomas Straub.)

During the 1990s, the old fermenting tanks were replaced by their newer stainless steel counterparts. Here, the first new fermenting tank arrives via crane. The brewery has 12 fermenting tanks located on three different floors in three different, specifically designated fermenting rooms labeled A, B, and C, which are located behind five-inch-thick doors. (Photograph by Thomas Straub.)

These are the storage tanks from the 1940s. They were constructed of carbon steel with a glass lining. (Photograph by Ray Beimel.)

Three of the new stainless steel storage tanks are shown arriving in 1993. The truck is pulling on to Sorg Street, where the brewery is located. The street was named after Francis Sorg and his family. (Photograph by Thomas Straub.)

The fermenting process takes seven days, during which time the yeast will consume the fermentable sugars in the wort, producing beer and, as a by-product, carbon dioxide, which is collected and filtered. This is the carbon dioxide collection and purification unit. (Photograph by Thomas Straub.)

After the fermentation process is completed, the beer is transferred to a 38-degree cellar for aging and double filtering. The brewery's former filtering system is shown here. (Photograph by Thomas Straub.)

This new filter replaced the old filter in 2001. During primary filtration, which is called roughing, and secondary filtration, which is called polishing, the filtered carbon dioxide is injected into the beer. (Photograph by Thomas Straub.)

Finally, the beer is transferred to either the racking room, where it is hand-racked or placed into kegs, or to the bottling house. Here, returned kegs are being washed and readied for use again in the keg washer around 1997. This machine was replaced in 2005. (Photograph by Thomas Straub.)

This is the top of the racking machine where the beer flows down into the kegs. (Courtesy of Straub Brewery.)

In this photograph, Peter's great-great-grandson Michael Maloney and Peter Bosnik are racking. (Courtesy of Straub Brewery.)

This is the bottling plant that was originally added in 1940. (Courtesy of Straub Brewery.)

In this *c.* 1972 photograph, brewery employee George Lucanik inspects the empty bottles after they come out of the bottle washer and before they are filled, pulling out any bottles that are not clean. (Photograph by Ray Beimel.)

Straub beer and Straub Light are bottled in eight-hour shifts. The bottles make a 45-minute journey along a conveyor belt, where they are rinsed, filled, capped, and labeled. This is a bottle filler from the 1950s. (Photograph by Ray Beimel.)

This is the filler, capping machine, and pasteurizer around 1983. (Photograph by Ray Beimel.)

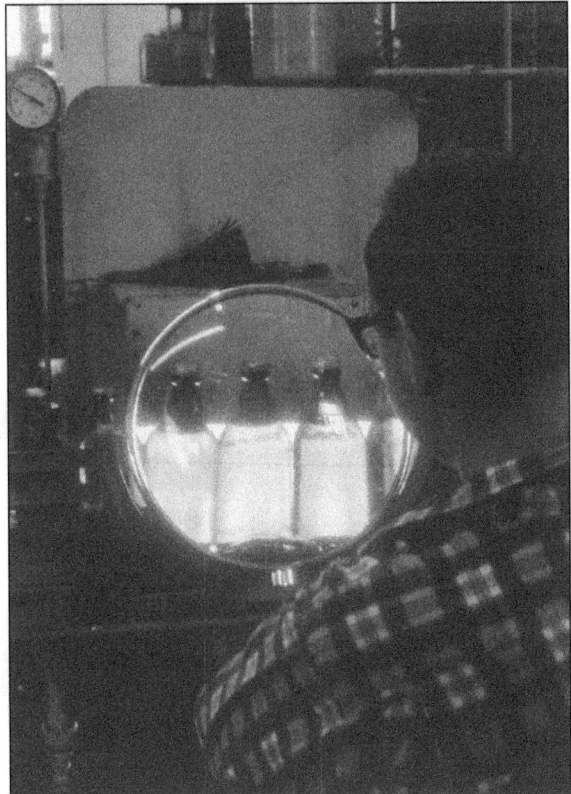

In this c. 1972 photograph, Jim Straub inspects the filled bottles to make sure that they are properly filled and that there is no dirt in them. He also checks for clarity. (Photograph by Ray Beimel.)

During the 45-minute journey, the bottles are, among other things, pasteurized as a slow warm-water drip gradually warms the beer from 38 degrees to 140 degrees. This is the old pasteurizer in action. (Courtesy of Straub Brewery.)

Here, the new stainless steel pasteurizer arrives in 1989. (Photograph by Thomas Straub.)

This is the old labeler around 1989. At this time, the brewery became one of the first to use a Videojet unit to put an open date code on bottles so that consumers know when the beer was produced. This code includes the month, day, and year of production, as well as the initials of the labeling machine operator. The new Krones labeler was delivered in 1996. (Photograph by Thomas Straub.)

This bottle washer from the mid-1900s was replaced in 1984. (Courtesy of Straub Brewery.)

Peter's grandson-in-law Ed Bosnik fills the beer cases by hand, picking up four bottles at a time to do so. The photograph was taken around 1972. (Photograph by Ray Beimel.)

The spent grain from the brewing process is being dumped into the back of a truck. The brewery sells the spent grain to farmers, who then use it as feed for their animals. (Photograph by Ray Beimel.)

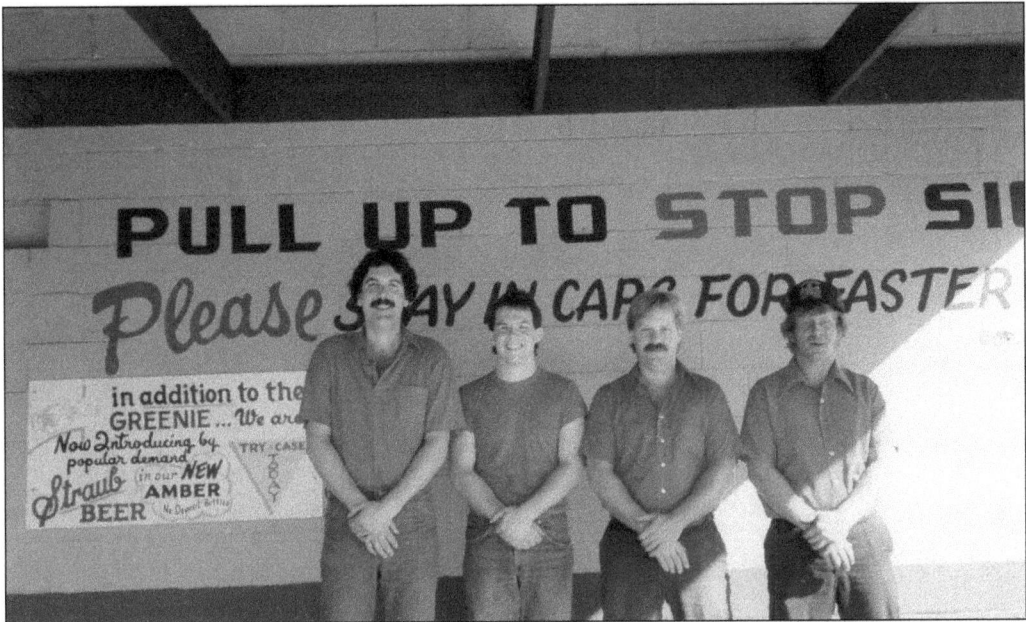

A large part of the Straub Brewery's business is done face-to-face at the drive-up store at the front of the brewery. Shown around 1984 are, from left to right, Dave Martin, Paul Taylor (Fr. Paul Taylor, O.S.B.), Steve Herzing, and Don Mahovlich. (Courtesy of Straub Brewery.)

The Eternal Tap, one of most popular sites at the brewery, is located just outside of the production area. Visitors are invited to enjoy a complimentary taste of the house brew. Originally, this beer was served in tin cups. Today, the tin cups have been replaced with glass mugs, but Straub beer continues to perpetually flow and satisfy local, national, and international visitors. (Photograph by JES II.)

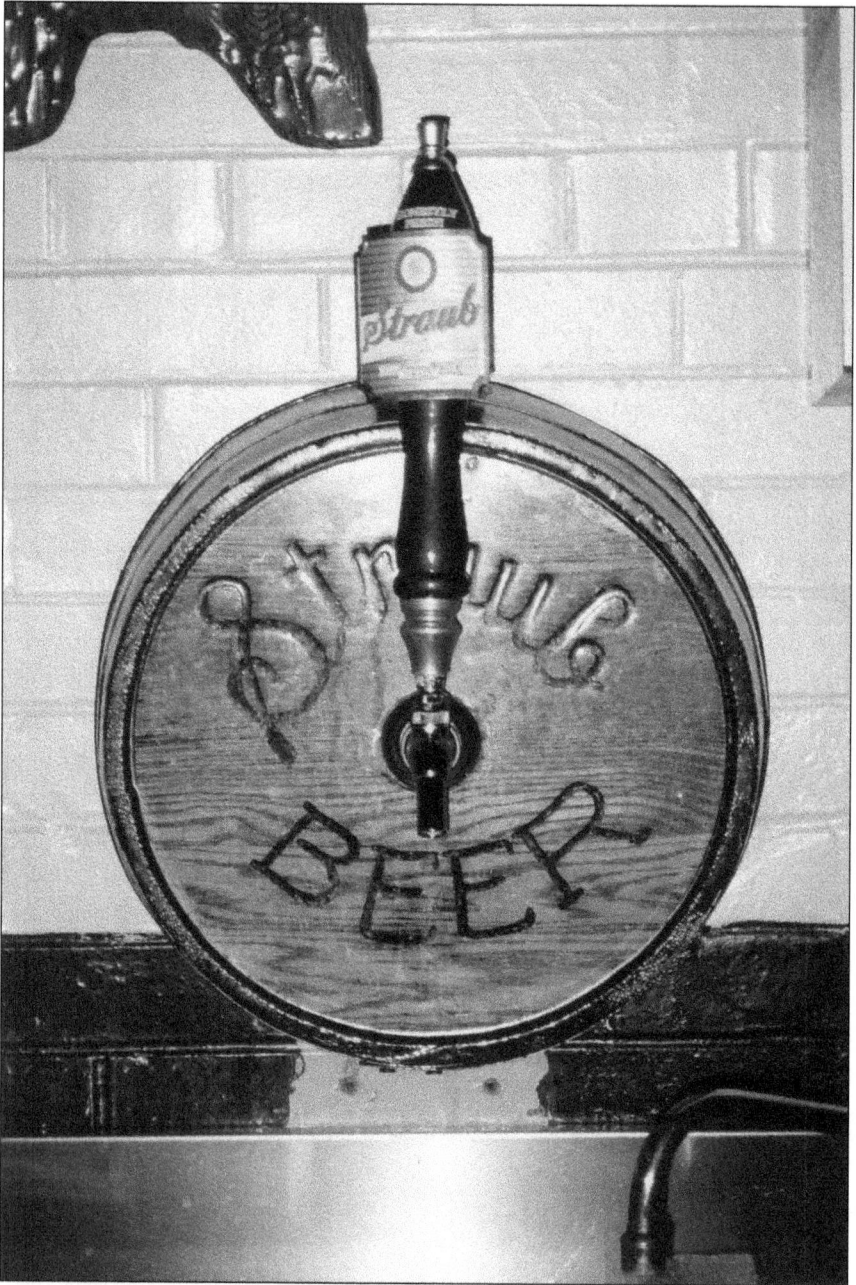

"Another legend has to do with another kind of locally prized gold—beer—that is said to flow freely and forever, a la the Fountain of Youth, from something called 'the Eternal Tap.' Thirsty souls seek the tap near the center of St. Marys, and usually find it. The Eternal Tap is real." —Bob Batz Jr., *Pittsburgh Press Sunday Magazine*, March 1, 1992.

An Associated Press article by Kelly P. Kissell sent news of the Eternal Tap around the world in 1993, garnering stories in such newspapers as the *Maui News* in Hawaii, *Salem Evening News* in Massachusetts, the *Orlando Sentinel* in Florida, the *Saginaw News* in Michigan, and the *Toronto Star* in Canada. Since then, numerous other media outlets have spread word of this iconic breweriana attraction. (Photograph by JES II.)

Four

ROLL OUT THE BARREL

"Never buy a cold case of beer and let it warm up and again chill it. Clean glasses are ever so important for a good tasting beer. Clean draught beer lines are again important. Never freeze beer. Proper bottle openers are required. Never expose beer to light. Especially to sunlight." —*History of the Straub Brewery*, 1980s.

Gilbert Straub pours a Straub's at the Flat Camp in Straub Bear Run around 1960. He always said, "You can tell if a beer is fresh because it always leaves a white ring on the inside of the glass." (Courtesy of JES II.)

Judging from these vintage beer caps, Straub's may not have been the only beverage at this party, but it was clearly the favorite. (Courtesy of Straub Brewery.)

Straub beer has also been known by consumers as "High Test" since the alcohol content is a little greater than in most beers. (Photograph by JES II, courtesy of Straub Brewery.)

Up until 1974, Straub beer was packaged only in amber-colored bottles. One day, the supplier accidentally sent nonreturnable green bottles. Rather than return the green bottles, the brewery decided to give them a try. They were an immediate success with patrons, giving birth to the Greenie. This promotional picture, taken at a later date, shows the Greenie proudly taking its place amongst the amber-colored bottles. (Courtesy of Straub Brewery.)

Today, Straub Light is available in 12-ounce nonreturnable amber bottles while Straub beer is available in 12- and 16-ounce returnable amber bottles as well as 12-ounce nonreturnable amber bottles and 12-ounce nonreturnable green bottles. As evidence of the public's affinity for one color over the other, Greenies account for approximately 70 percent of nonreturnable bottle sales. (Courtesy of Straub Brewery.)

Straub Light was introduced to the public on April 15, 1987. (Photograph by JES II, courtesy of Straub Brewery.)

Straub beer is a pilsner-type lager. According to the Brewers' Association of America's March 1969 "What a Brewery Salesman *Must* Know About His Product," *lager* is derived from the German verb meaning "to stock." (Photograph by JES II, courtesy of Straub Brewery.)

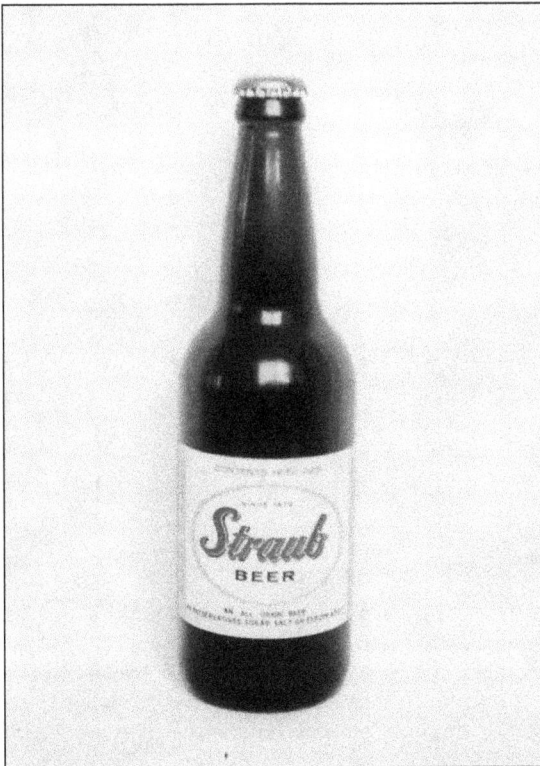

A 12-ounce bottle of Straub beer contains 128 calories, 3.45 percent alcohol by weight, 4.33 percent alcohol by volume, 10.1 grams of carbohydrates, 1.1 grams of protein, 0 grams of cholesterol, 0 grams of fat, .07 parts per million of iron, and .06 parts per million of sodium. (Photograph by JES II, courtesy of Straub Brewery.)

Twelve ounces of Straub Light contain 96 calories, 2.48 percent alcohol by weight, 3.16 percent alcohol by volume, 7.16 grams of carbohydrates, 1.1 grams of protein, 0 grams of cholesterol, 0 grams of fat, .05 parts per million of iron, and .06 parts per million of sodium. (Photograph by Ray Beimel.)

Always wanting to make life easier for its customers, the brewery created plastic bags not only for the convenience of carrying beer bottles but also for fishermen so they could put their fresh catch in the bags and even tie them to the side of the boat to keep cold while they enjoyed a Straub's. (Courtesy of Straub Brewery.)

This is a Straub Bock Beer bottle produced during the first half of the 1900s. (Photograph by JES II, courtesy of Straub Brewery.)

INTERNAL REVENUE TAX PAID

CONTENTS 12 FLUID OZ.

BOCK BEER

STRAUB BREWERY INC.

ST. MARYS, PA.

This is a Straub Bock Beer label that was used during the first half of the 1900s. (Courtesy of the Historical Society of St. Marys and Benzinger Township.)

Approximately 350,000 cases of Straub beer and Straub Light are produced annually. Straub beer bottle labels have changed many times since the bottling plant was added to the brewery in 1940. This is a 1950s label design for a quart bottle. (Courtesy of Straub Brewery.)

Approximately 2,000 cases of Straub beer and Straub Light are packaged during one day of production. St. Marys historian Alice Beimel remembers during the 1940s how the nuns, who were teachers, would recycle the extra Straub beer labels by having their students write their lessons on the blank backsides. This is a label design from the 1970s. (Courtesy of Straub Brewery.)

74

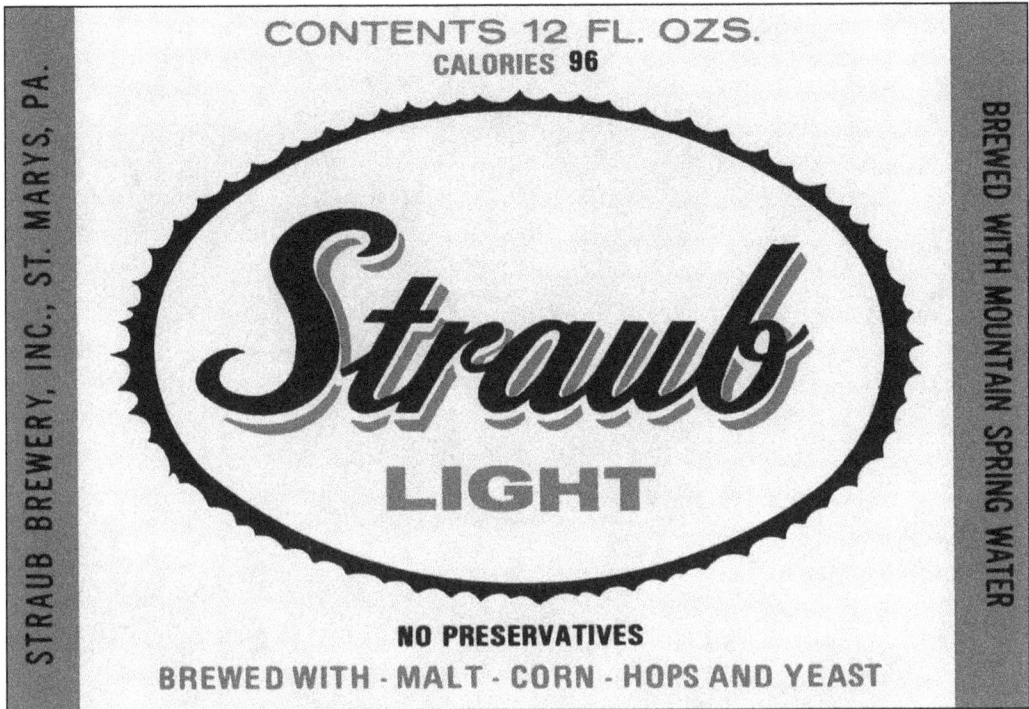

CONTENTS 12 FL. OZS.
CALORIES 96

STRAUB BREWERY, INC., ST. MARYS, PA.

Straub

LIGHT

BREWED WITH MOUNTAIN SPRING WATER

NO PRESERVATIVES
BREWED WITH · MALT · CORN · HOPS AND YEAST

Approximately 8,400,000 bottles of Straub beer and Straub Light are produced annually. Many people and groups have created their own labels for Straub beer bottles for special events, including class reunions and birthday parties. This is a Straub Light bottle label design from the late 1980s. (Courtesy of Straub Brewery.)

Approximately 48,000 bottles of Straub beer and Straub Light are filled during one day of production. The Straub family has created personalized labels for a variety of special events, including the ordination of Fr. Paul Taylor and Aunt Reggie's 100th birthday party. This is a Straub Light bottle label design from the late 1980s and 1990s. (Courtesy of Straub Brewery.)

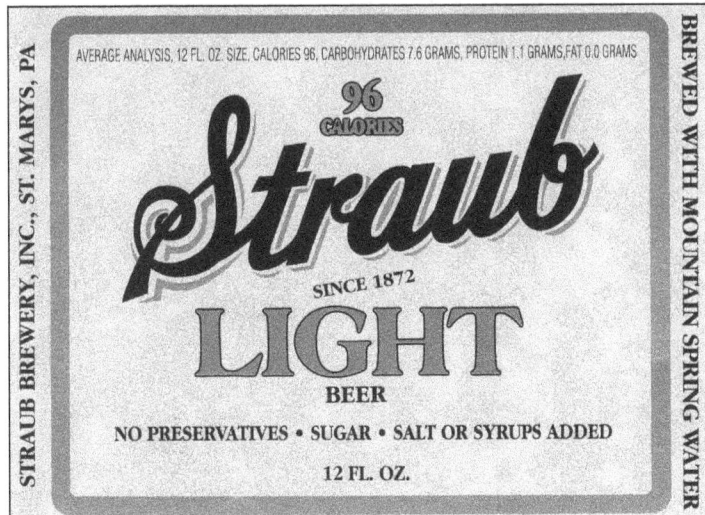

AVERAGE ANALYSIS, 12 FL. OZ. SIZE, CALORIES 96, CARBOHYDRATES 7.6 GRAMS, PROTEIN 1.1 GRAMS, FAT 0.0 GRAMS

STRAUB BREWERY, INC., ST. MARYS, PA

BREWED WITH MOUNTAIN SPRING WATER

96 CALORIES

Straub

SINCE 1872

LIGHT

BEER

NO PRESERVATIVES · SUGAR · SALT OR SYRUPS ADDED

12 FL. OZ.

Approximately 130 Straub beer and Straub Light bottles are filled during every minute of production. This is a metallic foil Straub beer bottle label design from the 1990s. One of the interesting details to note in the evolution of the labels is how the font of the Straub name changes, especially the S. (Courtesy of Straub Brewery.)

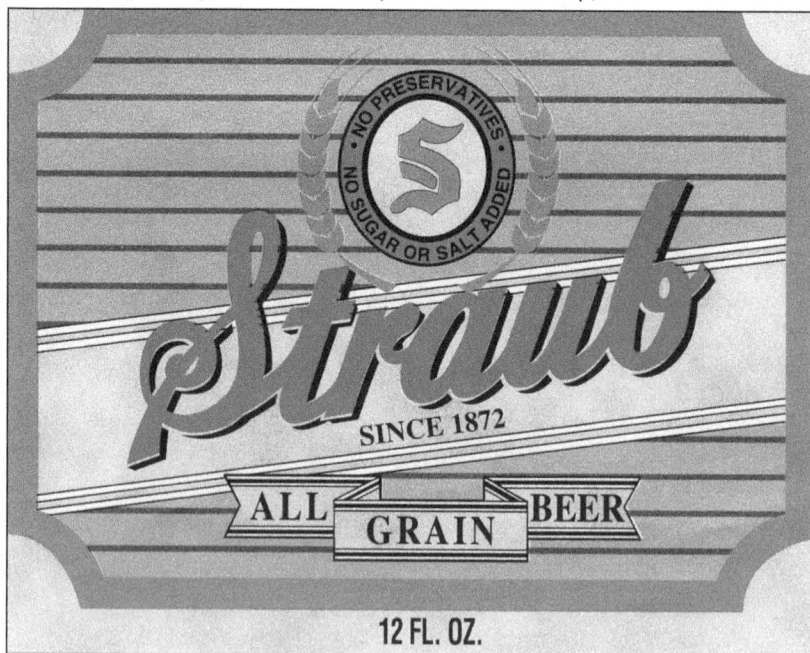

One barrel of Straub beer or Straub Light is equivalent to 31 gallons. This is a Straub beer bottle label design from the 1990s, which has a faux metallic design and is based on the original design that had a metallic sheen. (Courtesy of Straub Brewery.)

A half-barrel of Straub beer or Straub Light, including the keg, weighs approximately 160 pounds. This is a faux metallic Straub beer bottle label design from the 1990s. The various sizes of the labels, especially labels containing the same basic design such as this label and the two previous labels, make Straub beer bottles and labels sought-after collectibles among Straub drinkers and general breweriana enthusiasts. (Courtesy of Straub Brewery.)

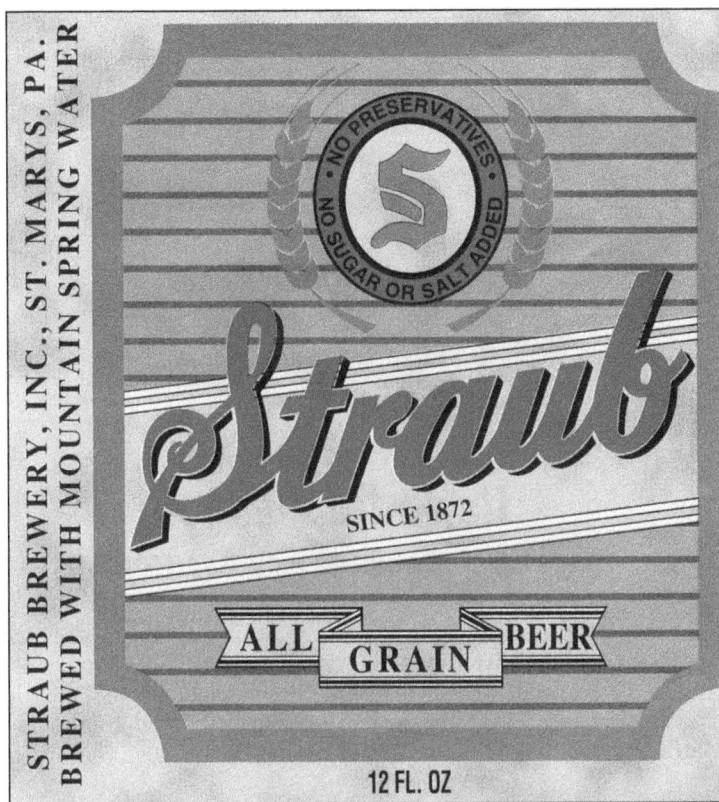

STRAUB BREWERY, INC., ST. MARYS, PA.
BREWED WITH MOUNTAIN SPRING WATER

NO PRESERVATIVES • NO SUGAR OR SALT ADDED

5

Straub

SINCE 1872

ALL GRAIN BEER

12 FL. OZ.

STRAUB BREWERY, INC., St MARYS, PA.
BREWED WITH MOUNTAIN SPRING WATER

AVERAGE ANALYSIS. PER 12 FL. OZ.: CALORIES 132, CARBOHYDRATES 10.5 GRAMS,
PROTEIN 1.3 GRAMS, FAT 0.0 GRAMS.

NO SALT, NO SUGAR, NO PRESERVATIVES ADDED

SINCE 1872

Straub

Beer in all its glory!
No sugar, No salt, No preservatives added.

12 FL. OZ.

GOVERNMENT WARNING: (1) ACCORDING TO THE SURGEON GENERAL, WOMEN SHOULD NOT DRINK ALCOHOLIC BEVERAGES DURING PREGNANCY BECAUSE OF THE RISK OF BIRTH DEFECTS. (2) CONSUMPTION OF ALCOHOLIC BEVERAGES IMPAIRS YOUR ABILITY TO DRIVE A CAR OR OPERATE MACHINERY, AND MAY CAUSE HEALTH PROBLEMS.

Approximately 36,000 barrels of Straub beer and Straub Light are produced annually. This is a Straub beer bottle label design from the late 1990s, which boasts one of the product's slogans, "Beer in all its glory!" It even has the little Bavarian Straub Beer Man at the top in gold. (Courtesy of Straub Brewery.)

STRAUB BREWERY, INC., ST MARYS, PA. BREWED WITH MOUNTAIN SPRING WATER

AVERAGE ANALYSIS, PER 12 FL. OZ., CALORIES 96, CARBOHYDRATES 7.6 GRAMS, PROTEIN 1.1 GRAMS, FAT 0.0 GRAMS

NO SALT, NO SUGAR, NO PRESERVATIVES ADDED

SINCE 1872

Straub

LIGHT

Honestly Fresh All Grain Beer

No sugar, No salt, No preservatives added.

96 CALORIES

12 FL. OZ.

Approximately 145 barrels or 4,500 gallons of Straub beer and Straub Light are produced during one day of brewing. This is a recent Straub Light bottle label design that boasts one of the product's slogans, "Honestly Fresh All Grain Beer," and also has the little Bavarian Straub Beer Man at the top in gold. (Courtesy of Straub Brewery.)

One of the most significant changes to the label designs has been the addition of a neck label on bottles, which is seen on this Straub beer bottle in the mid-1900s. Over the years, neck labels have come and gone and then come back again. (Photograph by JES II, courtesy of Straub Brewery.)

THE OFFICIAL LIGHT BEER OF GROUNDHOG DAY 2000

AVERAGE ANALYSIS, 12 FL. OZ. SIZE, CALORIES 96, CARBOHYDRATES 7.6 GRAMS, PROTEIN 1.1 GRAMS, FAT 0.0 GRAMS

GROUNDHOG BREW

12 FLUID OUNCES • LIGHT BEER
BREWED WITH MOUNTAIN SPRING WATER
STRAUB BREWERY, INC., ST. MARYS, PA.

GOVERNMENT WARNING: (1) ACCORDING TO THE SURGEON GENERAL, WOMEN SHOULD NOT DRINK ALCOHOLIC BEVERAGES DURING PREGNANCY BECAUSE OF THE RISK OF BIRTH DEFECTS. (2) CONSUMPTION OF ALCOHOLIC BEVERAGES IMPAIRS YOUR ABILITY TO DRIVE A CAR OR OPERATE MACHINERY, AND MAY CAUSE HEALTH PROBLEMS.

In 2000, to commemorate Groundhog Day, the brewery joined forces with the Punxsutawney Groundhog Club in Punxsutawney, Pennsylvania, to create an annual limited 3,000 or less case edition of Straub Light called Groundhog Brew. This is the first Groundhog Brew bottle label. (Courtesy of Straub Brewery.)

During the 1990s, the brewery assumed the pseudonyms Crooked Creek Brewery and Pymatuning Dam Brewery to produce Dam Beer for the Pymatuning Dam in Jamestown, Pennsylvania. This is a Dam Beer bottle label from the 1990s. (Courtesy of Straub Brewery.)

79

AVERAGE ANALYSIS, 12FL. OZ. SIZE, CALORIES 96, CARBOHYDRATES 7.6 GRAMS, PROTEIN 1.1 GRAMS, FAT 0.0 GRAMS

zipLight™

A bright, light beer

Beer

12 FL. OZ

GOVERNMENT WARNING : (1) ACCORDING TO THE SURGEON GENERAL, WOMEN SHOULD NOT DRINK ALCOHOLIC BEVERAGES DURING PREGNANCY BECAUSE OF THE RISK OF BIRTH DEFECTS. (2) CONSUMPTION OF ALCOHOLIC BEVERAGES IMPAIRS YOUR ABILITY TO DRIVE A CAR OR OPERATE MACHINERY, AND MAY CAUSE HEALTH PROBLEMS.

Brewed with mountain spring water by Straub Brewery, Inc.,

In 2000, the brewery teamed with the Bradford, Pennsylvania–based Zippo Manufacturing Company to produce the official beer for the Zippo/Case International Swap Meet, held on July 21 and 22, 2000. (Courtesy of Straub Brewery.)

OUR GUARANTEE

SINCE 1889

W. R. Case & Sons

Brewed by a process known only to ourselves

12FL. OZ.

SELECT BEER

GOVERNMENT WARNING : (1) ACCORDING TO THE SURGEON GENERAL, WOMEN SHOULD NOT DRINK ALCOHOLIC BEVERAGES DURING PREGNANCY BECAUSE OF THE RISK OF BIRTH DEFECTS. (2) CONSUMPTION OF ALCOHOLIC BEVERAGES IMPAIRS YOUR ABILITY TO DRIVE A CAR OR OPERATE MACHINERY, AND MAY CAUSE HEALTH PROBLEMS.

Brewed with mountain spring water by Straub Brewery, Inc., just over the hill in St. Marys, PA.

This W. R. Case & Sons Select Beer bottle label was also created for the Zippo/Case International Swap Meet. The bearded gentlemen used in the Case trademark and seen on this label is Job Case, the grandfather of Case founder John Russell Case. Case is now owned by Zippo. (Courtesy of Straub Brewery.)

80

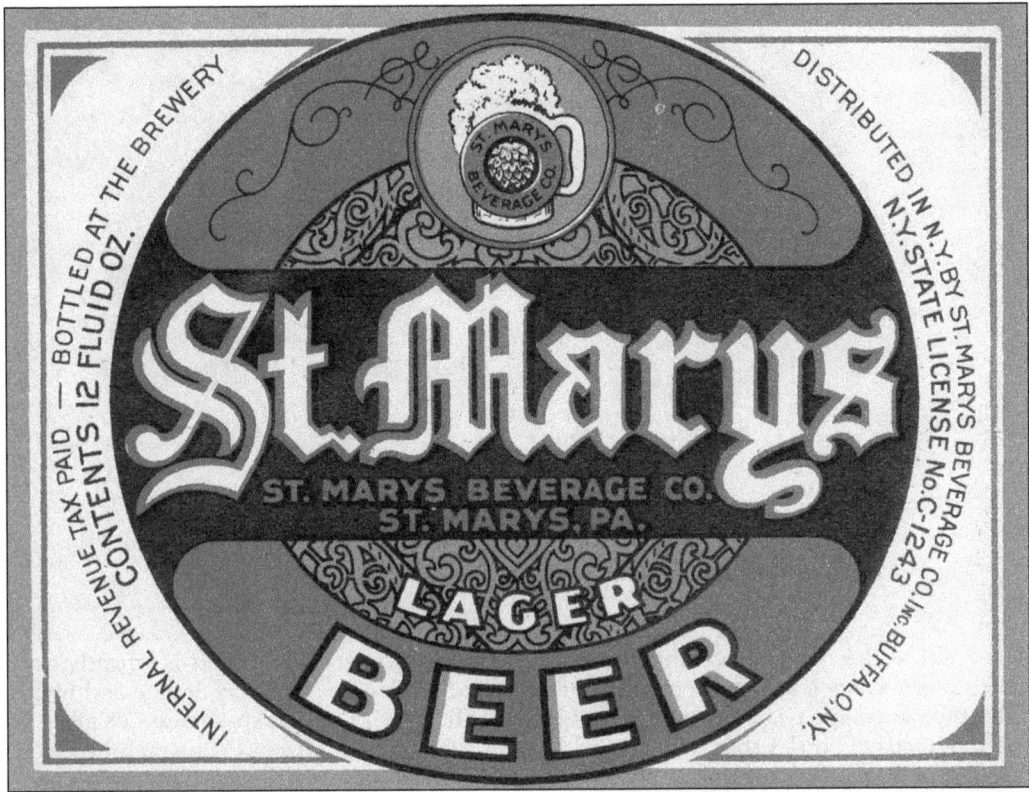

This is a rare St. Marys Beer label from the St. Marys Beverage Company from the early 1900s. (Courtesy of Straub Brewery.)

When it comes to labels, the brewery is not only willing to get personal, but it also has a sense of humor, especially regarding family. This special label, proclaiming, "Family in all its glory" and spoofing one of the product's slogans, was created for the sixth Straub family reunion on July 1, 2000. (Courtesy of JES II.)

The brewery's beer cases have undergone some changes over the years. This is an early case, which was a wooden box that proudly displayed the Straub name in red. The rare and highly collectible wooden cases show the fruits of labor in the form of well-worn impressions made by the thousands of bottles that were carried in each case over the years. (Photograph by JES II, courtesy of Straub Brewery.)

When the brewery made St. Marys Little Dutchman Premium Beer in the 1960s, this special case was used for that particular brew. (Photograph by JES II, courtesy of Straub Brewery.)

The newest case designs for Straub beer come in red and green. The cases for Straub Light come in gold, and each displays a rendering of the 1895 brewery in the background. (Photograph by JES II, courtesy of Straub Brewery.)

This case design for the plastic bottles bears vintage-looking, faded red lettering against white. In addition to the glass bottles, the brewery started to use plastic bottles for Straub beer in January 2001. (Photograph by JES II, courtesy of Straub Brewery.)

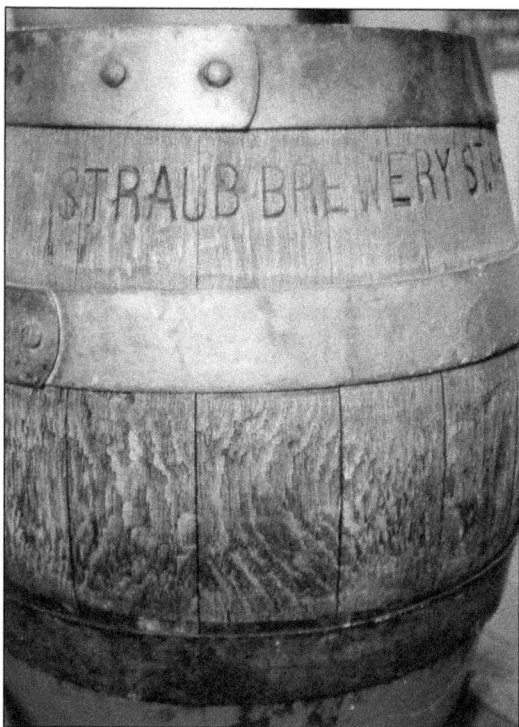

Peter Straub used wooden kegs for his beer. He always placed a red band around his barrels to ensure that people would know they were drinking his beer and so that he would get them back. As a lasting trademark tribute to Peter, the brewery continues to place a bright red band around each of its barrels. Red has become a trademark color for the brewery. (Photograph by JES II, courtesy of Straub Brewery.)

This is the top of a wooden keg used by the Peter Straub Sons Brewery in the early 1900s. (Photograph by JES II, courtesy of Straub Brewery.)

The brewery eventually replaced the wooden kegs with aluminum and stainless steel kegs. These kegs have a Hoff-Stevens tapping system, meaning they have a two-prong system that is filled through a bung hole. Stacks of kegs can be found throughout the brewery, even at the foot of the stairs leading to the brewmaster's office. (Photograph by JES II.)

Today's brewery does not rely on the traditional red band alone to signify its brew; the keg cap also bears the brewery's name. This keg design was discontinued in 2005. (Photograph by JES II.)

In April 2005, the brewery changed its longtime keg, opting for a more streamlined design with a Sankey tapping system. The Sankey tapping system has a single port and ball apparatus that allows for easy cleaning and filling. Yet one more era in the brewery's history began. (Photograph by JES II.)

Five

SERVING UP STRAUB'S

"A clever ad man might take the Straub Beer account and promote the frothy brew as a new cult phenomenon, the all-organic, all-natural beer that contains no sugar, no additives, no preservatives—just pure ingredients and sparkling Elk County spring water." —Geoffrey Tomb, *Post-Gazette Daily Magazine*, September 22, 1977.

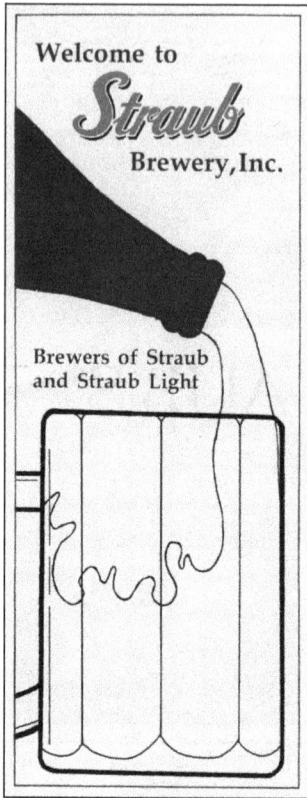

The brewery's best advertising campaigns have always been the satisfied customers' word of mouth. A number of brochures have been created and distributed by the brewery over the years, including this Straub Brewery brochure from the late 1980s. (Courtesy of Straub Brewery.)

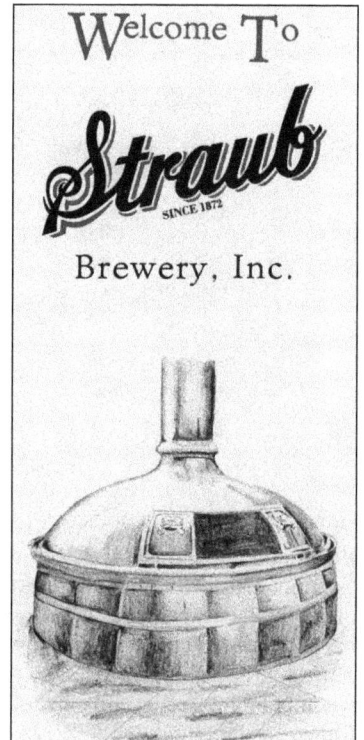

This is a Straub Brewery brochure from the late 1980s. (Courtesy of Straub Brewery.)

This is a Straub Brewery brochure from the early 1990s. (Courtesy of Straub Brewery.)

Pictured is another early-1990s brochure. (Courtesy of Straub Brewery.)

This brochure dates from the late 1990s. (Courtesy of Straub Brewery.)

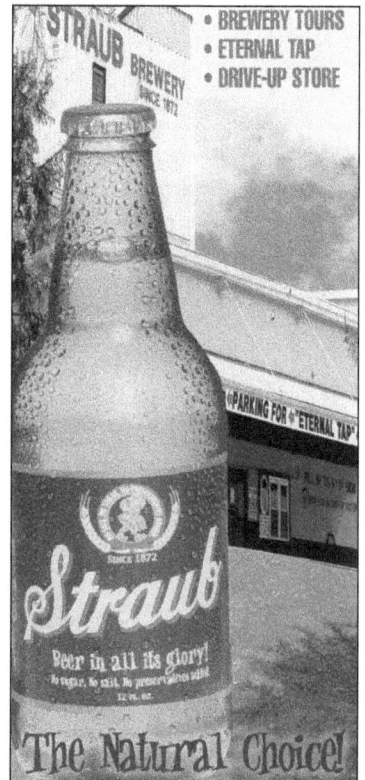

This is a newer Straub Brewery brochure. (Courtesy of Straub Brewery.)

Rather than give in to the "sex sells" mentality like other larger breweries, the Straub Brewery chose instead to celebrate the wildlife that has become synonymous with the town and county in which the brewery is located, most strikingly portrayed in this mid-1990s poster of an elk and young deer meeting nose to nose. (Courtesy of Straub Brewery.)

HONESTLY FRESH!

Straub

and *Straub* Light
all Natural ... all Grain Beers !

Brewed by Straub Brewery, Inc. — St. Marys, Pennsylvania

STRAUB

A WISE CHOICE

Bock Beer

STRAUB BREWERY INC. ST. MARYS, PA

When the brewery produced Straub Bock Beer during the first half of the 1900s, this vintage poster from the 1940s helped to promote the product throughout the area. Bock Beer is a heavier and usually darker beer with a strong malt, yet sweet taste. (Courtesy of Straub Brewery.)

The brewery has launched a few characters throughout its history. The fuzzy little green character in this mid-1980s poster is encouraging patrons to "have a Greenie!" (Courtesy of Straub Brewery.)

The little green man was brought back in this poster from the late 1980s to help promote the debut of Straub Light by encouraging drinkers to "expose yourself to a new light beer." (Courtesy of Straub Brewery.)

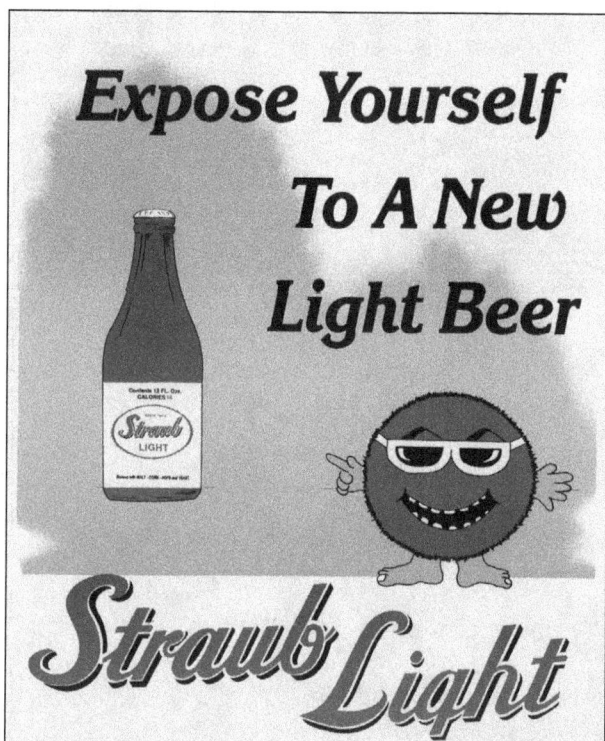

This festive poster helps celebrate the brewery's 125 years in the business and emphasizes the unique open date coding on every bottle. The little Bavarian Straub Beer Man seen in the upper right-hand corner of the poster has been an iconic and heritage-based trademark image for the brewery for decades and continues to be a popular feature on brewery merchandise. (Courtesy of Straub Brewery.)

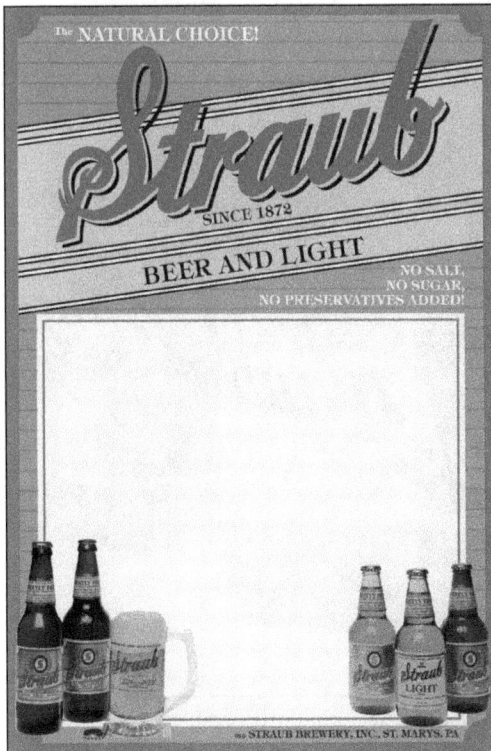

This poster from the 1990s relies heavily on the visual of the thirst-quenching and earthy marvel that is Straub beer, advertising the brew as "the Natural Choice." (Courtesy of Straub Brewery.)

This poster from 2005 places an emphasis on brand name and pure product. (Courtesy of Straub Brewery.)

Six

CELEBRATING, STRAUB-STYLE

"Bud is Bud and light is light, but Straub's is Pennsylvania." —Gov. Robert P. Casey, St. Marys Capital for a Day press conference (excerpted from the *Daily Press*, October 2, 1992).

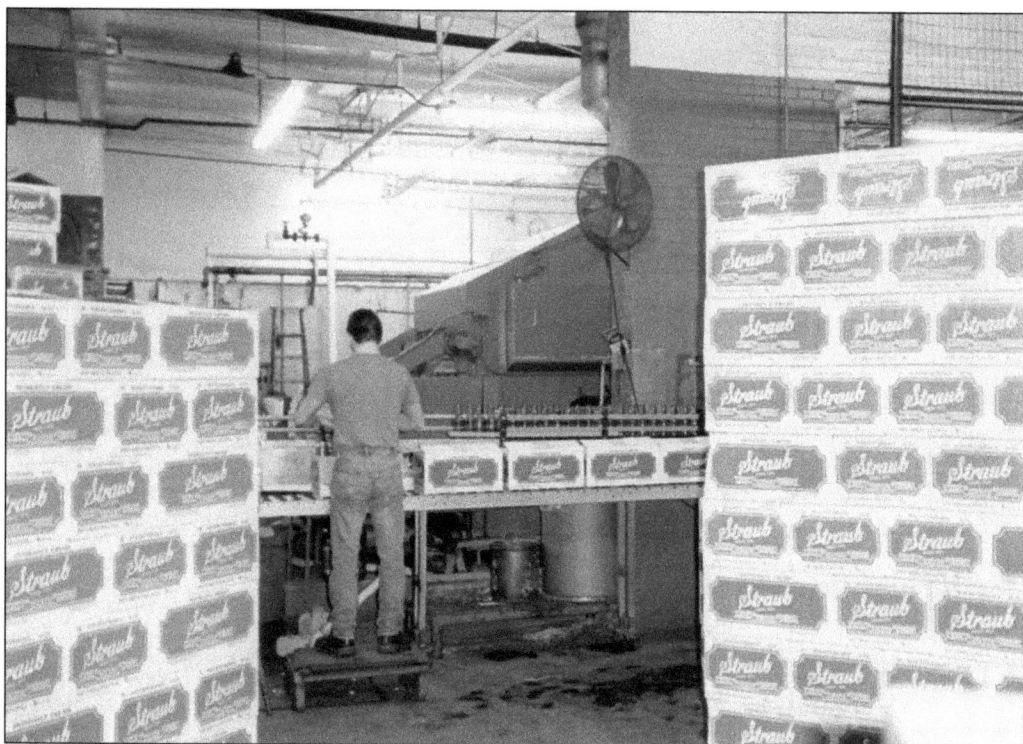

In May 1980, Michele Kuhar, from the Division of Film Promotion of the Pennsylvania Department of Commerce, expressed interest in using the brewery as a location for a comedy film based on Johnny Paycheck's legendary song "Take This Job and Shove It." Kuhar's letter stated, "The location request requires a working brewery situated in a small town." (Photograph by JES II.)

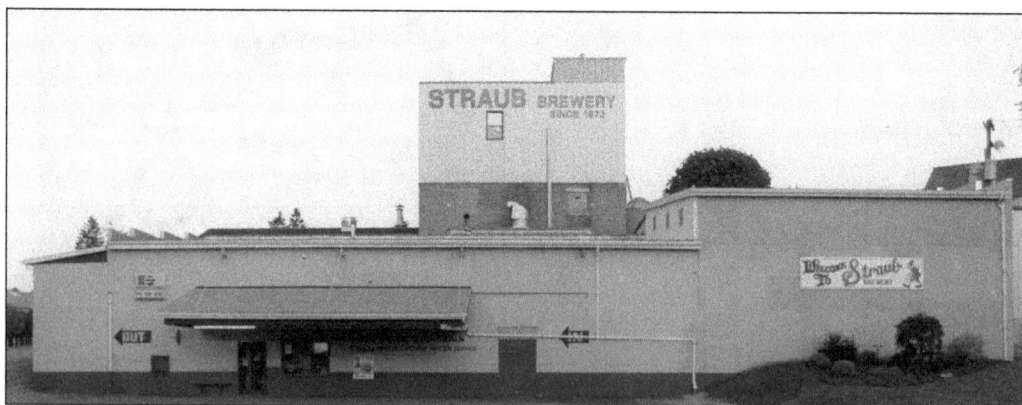

This is the Hollywood headshot that never was. In August 1980, location manager Michael Fottrell sent the brewery a letter explaining that *Take This Job and Shove It* was going to be filmed at the Joseph S. Pickett & Sons Brewery in Dubuque, Iowa, which had also been a site for the Sylvester Stallone flick *F.I.S.T.* (Photograph by Ray Beimel.)

Straub beer has yet to make it to the silver screen, but it has appeared on various news programs, in countless articles, in the novels *Winter in the Heart* (David Poyer) and *Convicted* (Megan Hart), and in *The Pennsylvania Celebrities Cookbook* and *The Ultimate Elk Cookbook*. However, brewery workers are more focused on creating their quality product than on what movie or book their brew may be in. (Photograph by JES II.)

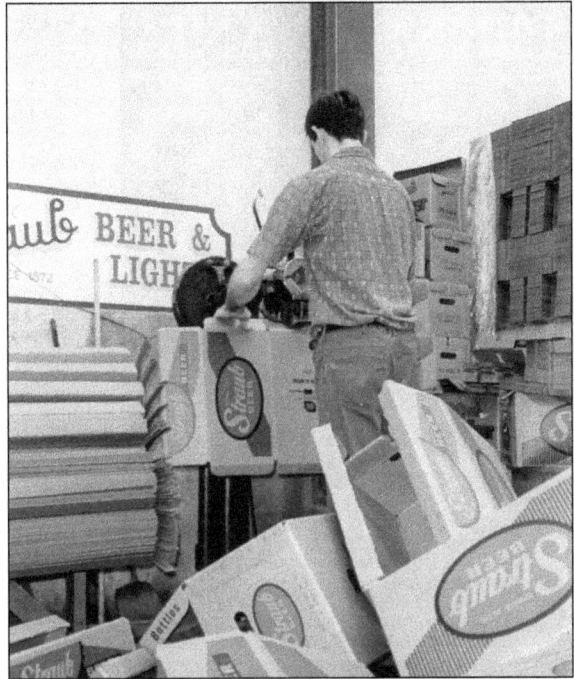

In 1994, Straub Light was chosen to be the best over 80 other light beers from 25 breweries—including the likes of Samuel Adams, Rolling Rock, Labatts U.S.A., Anheuser-Busch, Miller, Stroh's, and Coors—at the United States Beer and Music Festival, held at Station Square in Pittsburgh. This vintage bottle label reflects the brew's award-winning status. (Courtesy of Straub Brewery.)

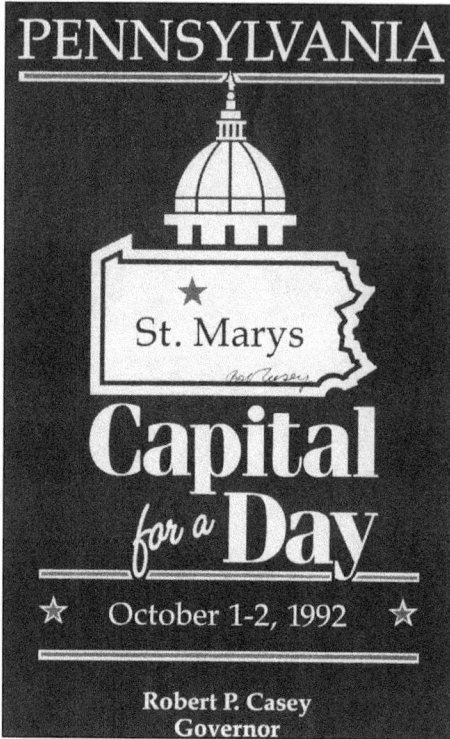

On October 1 and 2, 1992, St. Marys became Pennsylvania's capital for a day. This poster from the event is signed by Gov. Robert P. Casey. (Courtesy of JES II.)

Governor Casey visited the brewery during the two-day event. He inspected a bottle of Straub's along with Rep. Dan Surra and Dan Straub. (Photograph by Ray Beimel.)

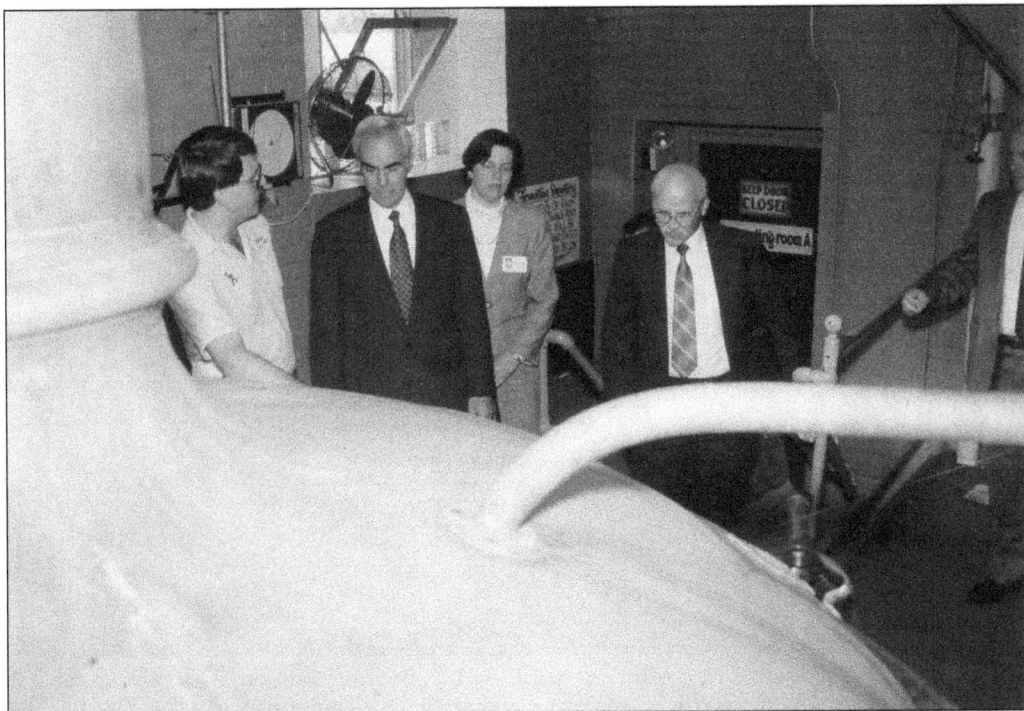

Gov. Robert P. Casey, along with Rep. Dan Surra, was introduced to the famous Copper Kettle by Thomas Straub. (Photograph by Ray Beimel.)

The governor and Thomas Straub enjoyed a taste of the house brew at the Eternal Tap while Rep. Dan Surra looked on. (Photograph by Ray Beimel.)

These special limited edition Straub beer steins are all about celebration. The one on the left displays the Victory Arch for the St. Marys welcome home celebration on August 7, 1919. The other stein combines elements from the 1895 brewery picture, including Peter, and the modern brewery. (Courtesy of Straub Brewery.)

In the early to mid-1900s, St. Marys hosted a few large parades, celebrating the holidays and local heritage. The brewery always played an important role in these festivities by entering elaborate floats. This float is from the Labor Day parade in 1934. (Courtesy of Ray Beimel.)

A brewery float boasts the message "Fire Prevention Every Day, Clean Up, Get Busy" on Brussells Street before it joins the welcome home parade for the World War I soldiers on August 7, 1919, when the entire town was celebrating and the last dance broke up at six the next morning. (Courtesy of Straub Brewery.)

A brewery float carries two large white elk in a 1950s parade. The elk on the float linked the area's favorite brew to another local attraction, the nearby and famous Pennsylvania elk herds. Also, the brewery is located in Elk County. It has always been important to the brewery to support and celebrate the local heritage and traditions. (Courtesy of JES II.)

The brewery's white elk make an appearance on this Benevolent Protection Order of Elks (BPOE) parade float around 1946 with a Straub banner placed on a Ford car in the background. (Photograph by John B. Cliff, courtesy of JES II.)

This was the brewery float for a firemen's parade in the 1940s. (Courtesy of JES II.)

Even the youngest paradegoers get to catch a ride on Straub's during the 125th anniversary celebration of the founding of St. Marys in 1967. (Photograph by Grotzinger Studio, courtesy of JES II.)

This was the brewery's horse-drawn wagon float in the St. Marys sesquicentennial parade in 1992. (Courtesy of Straub Brewery.)

The big Straub beer blow-up bottle is always a parade and party favorite. Here, the bottle marches onward during the St. Marys sesquicentennial parade in 1992. St. Marys historian and photographer Ray Beimel is seen recording the event. (Courtesy of Straub Brewery.)

Peter brings up the end on this horse-drawn brewery float for the 2000 firemen's parade, which celebrated the 100th anniversary of the local, volunteer St. Marys Fire Department. (Photograph by Thomas Straub.)

On December 8, 2002, Peter Straub was honored by the Historical Society of St. Marys and Benzinger Township as its Distinguished Citizen of 2002. This event culminated a year-long celebration of the brewery's 130th anniversary. This is the program from the event. (Courtesy of JES II.)

The 40th Annual Banquet of the Historical Society of St. Marys and Benzinger Township Commemorating The Founding of St. Marys on December 8, 1842

PRESENTED BY

THE HISTORICAL SOCIETY OF ST. MARYS AND BENZINGER TOWNSHIP

160th Anniversary of St. Marys
150th Anniversary of the Benedictine Sisterhood
130th Anniversary of Straub Brewery

Hors d'oeuvres
Straub Beer Fondue with Rye Bread ~Page 10~

Straub Beer Classic Dip ~Page 8~

Straub Beer Meatballs ~Page 12~

The Club's Green Goods with Dipping Sauce
~Chef's Original Choice~

Dinner
Straub Beer Dressing Over Green Salad ~Page 66~

Straub Beer Cabbage ~Page 74~

Straub Beer Garlic Roast Beef ~Page 114~

Straub Beer Ham ~Page 156~

The Club's Potato Pancakes
~Chef's Original Choice~

The Club's Dessert
~Chef's Original Choice~

STRAUB BEER FOOD FEST
~FRIDAY, NOVEMBER 5, 2004~

Selections from The Straub Beer Cookbook

On November 5, 2004, the Straub Beer Food Fest was held at the St. Marys Country Club. Guests were treated to a buffet of dishes prepared with Straub beer and inspired by *The Straub Beer Cookbook*. This program was patterned after menu cards used at the White House. Placemats were also designed using a picture of the Straub Brewery float from the Labor Day parade in 1934. (Courtesy of JES II.)

105

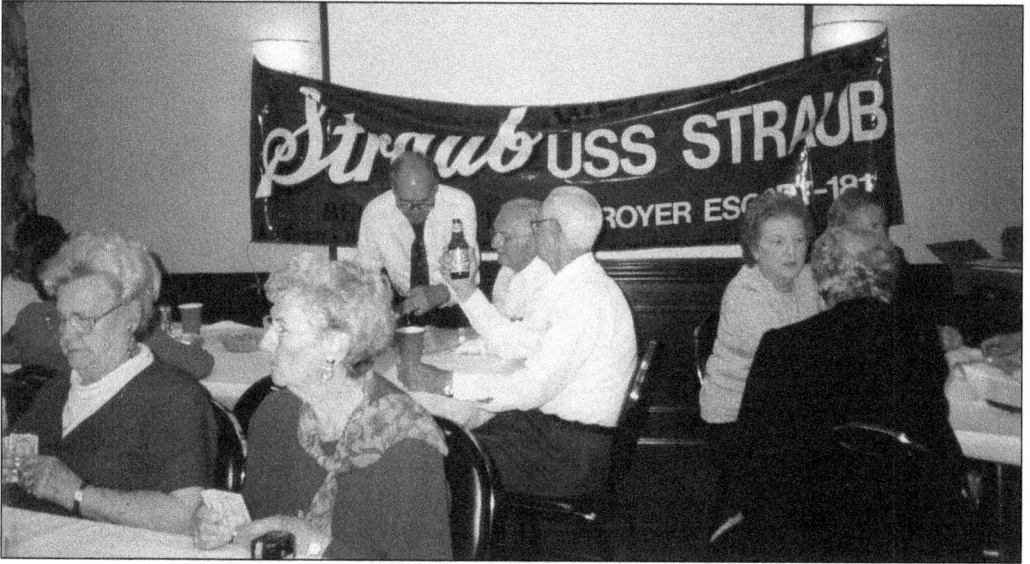

The destroyer USS *Straub* was not named after the St. Marys Straubs, but a friendly relationship developed between the crew and the brewery, as seen here at an October 17, 1998, crew reunion. (Courtesy of Straub Brewery.)

The brewery has always supported and sponsored many causes and events, including sports teams, the *Straub's Sports Parade* radio show, nonprofit organizations, and scholarships at the two local high schools. This is one of the Little League teams that have carried the brewery's name. To the far right is Peter's great-grandson coach Aaron Straub, and third from the left in the front is Peter's great-great-grandson Douglas Straub. (Courtesy of Straub Brewery.)

Since the late 1990s, the brewery has sponsored this car driven by Dom Surra, the son of Rep. Dan Surra. (Courtesy of Straub Brewery.)

For many years, the brewery has sponsored this car driven on the local racing circuit by Lauren Sallack. (Courtesy of Straub Brewery.)

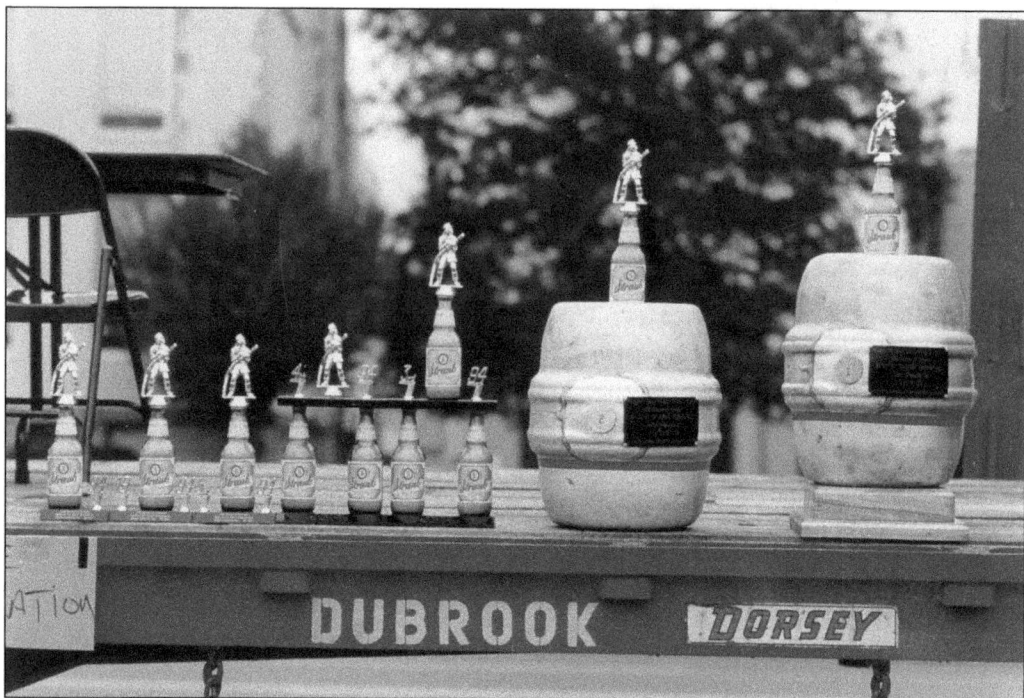

Straub beer literally became the trophies in this St. Marys Battle of the Barrel during the Hometown Festival in 1994. (Courtesy of Straub Brewery.)

Dan Straub (far left) and his teammates, from left to right, Dave Martin, Steve Herzing, and Don Mahovlich, took home the grand prize in the St. Marys 1985 keg-rolling competition. (Courtesy of Straub Brewery.)

This group portrait from the 1980s was taken at one of the many distributors picnics that the brewery hosted at Straub Bear Run. Second from the right in the back is John Skok, who took on the role of the brewery's second salesmen after Peter P. in the 1950s and then again in the 1970s. Similar picnics were also held for many years for brewery employees. (Courtesy of Straub Brewery.)

Artists have often used the brewery as a subject for paintings and other pieces. The most popular subject is the 1895 brewery image. Lynda M. Pontzer depicted the brewery scene in a 30-by-40-inch oil painting, adding in the photographer who snapped the shot. The painting was turned into this postcard and sold as part of a set with three other local scenes. (Artwork by Lynda M. Pontzer.)

Russ Brennen depicted the 1895 brewery in an 11-by-14-inch watercolor painting, which he eventually reproduced in a limited edition series of 250 art prints. (Artwork by Russ Brennen.)

Shirley Nicklas depicted the modern brewery in a 12-by-16-inch watercolor painting, which was eventually turned into this postcard and sold as part of the New Marienstadt Collection (1991), which also depicted other St. Marys landmarks. (Artwork by Shirley Nicklas.)

In 2002, to commemorate the 130th anniversary of the brewery, the world-famous Zippo Manufacturing Company teamed up with the brewery to create two special Zippo lighters and a Case knife, a project that was spearheaded by Bob Troha. This lighter bears the 1895 brewery image and was limited to 130 lighters. (Courtesy of Zippo Manufacturing Company.)

In 2002, W. R. Case & Sons Cutlery Company, owned by Zippo, produced a special pocket knife with a money clip bearing the image of the Bavarian Straub Beer Man. (Courtesy of Zippo Manufacturing Company.)

St. Marys train enthusiast Acky Herr created these miniature Straub pieces for his train set. (Photograph by Allen Herr.)

Seven

HAVE YOUR STRAUB'S AND EAT IT TOO

"Beer, to begin with, is a food. In Germany many songs and local proverbs link the name with bread. *Bier und Brot*. It is more to many drinkers in that it may be considered a specific against many of the ills of the body and mind. It is first a refresher and then a mild stimulant which wipes the cobwebs from dusty minds; it tones up the system, restores circulation, clears the eyes, and brings the rose back to faded cheeks."
—*Carbon Copy*, April 1942.

While operating as Straub Brothers Brewery during Prohibition, the brewery sold St. Mary's Special Malt Syrup, which many people used to make their own brew at home. This is a vintage can for the syrup. (Photograph by JES II, courtesy of the Historical Society of St. Marys and Benzinger Township.)

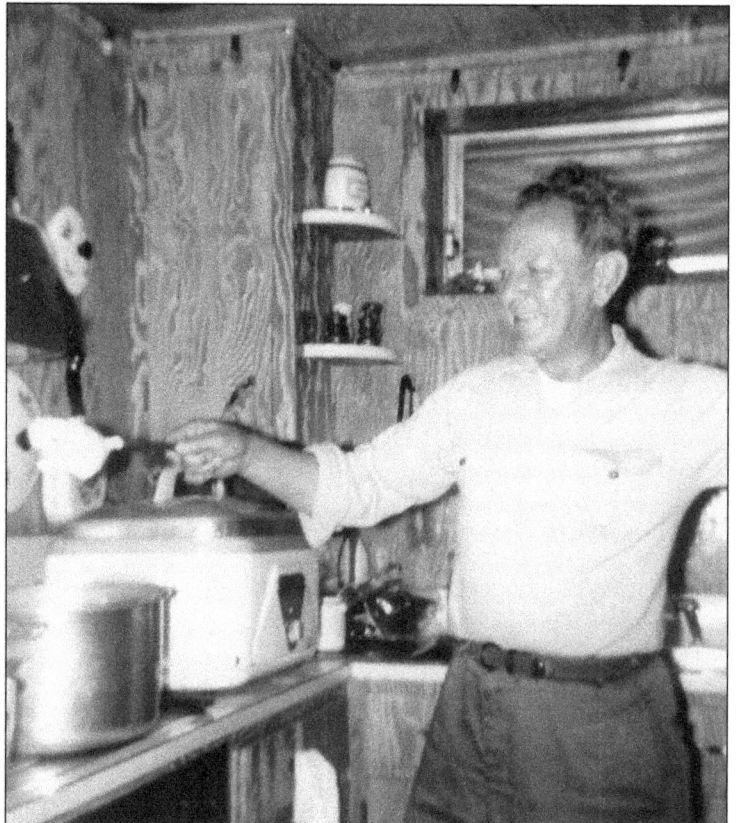

Former Straub brewmaster Gilbert Straub was always at home in the kitchen and loved entertaining family and friends. He was known for many of his dishes, including his Straub Beer Battered Shrimp. Here, Gilbert gets ready for a party in Straub Country around 1965. (Courtesy of Straub Brewery.)

STRAUB BROTHERS

ST. MARYS, PA.

Malt Pudding

2 cups whole wheat flour
1 cup milk
½ cup malt extract
1 cup raisins or other fruit
½ teaspoon salt

Mix salt with flour, add raisins or other fruit, and mix; then add milk and malt extract, and mix again. Steam in closed vessel for about three hours and serve with plain sauce or whipped cream.

This is the Malt Pudding recipe printed on the St. Mary's Special Malt Syrup can label. (Courtesy of the Historical Society of St. Marys and Benzinger Township.)

THE *Straub* BEER COOKBOOK

Recipes Selected, Edited, & Introduced By
JOHN E. SCHLIMM II

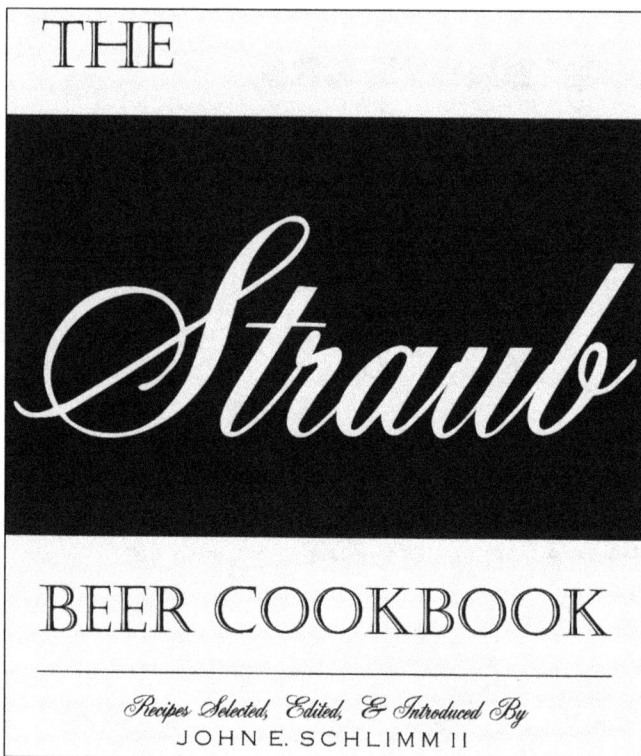

In 2003, *The Straub Beer Cookbook* was published. A copy was donated to the Pennsylvania Governor's Residence Library. In a note to the author, Pennsylvania's First Lady, Judge Midge Rendell, wrote, "It will certainly be a welcomed addition to the library. And, I am certain that the Residence chefs will be anxious to try out a few of the recipes for our sampling." (Courtesy of Stohn Books.)

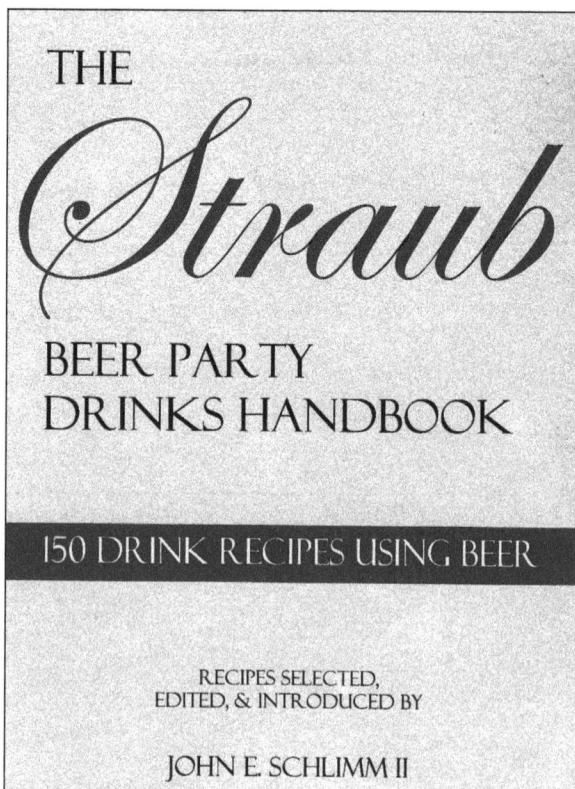

THE *Straub* BEER PARTY DRINKS HANDBOOK

150 DRINK RECIPES USING BEER

RECIPES SELECTED, EDITED, & INTRODUCED BY

JOHN E. SCHLIMM II

On December 6, 2004, the Associated Press blasted a story around the world, asking readers, "Want to Skip and Go Naked?" They were referring to one of the drinks in *The Straub Beer Party Drinks Handbook*. That story garnered pieces reported by print, radio, and television news from the eastern end of the United States to Hawaii and even into Canada and everywhere in between. (Courtesy of Stohn Books.)

Straub SINCE 1872 BEER & LIGHT

Write from the kettle...

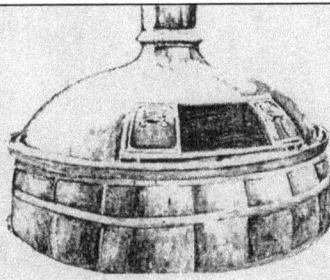

Straub Beer Garlic Roast Beef

Serves 10-12

4 pound beef top round roast
3/4 cup Straub Beer
2 tablespoons vegetable oil
2 cloves garlic (finely chopped)
1/2 teaspoon salt
1/8 teaspoon pepper
2 teaspoons instant beef bouillon
1/4 cup cold water
2 tablespoons all-purpose flour

Pierce the beef roast thouroughly with a fork. Place the beef in a glass bowl. In another bowl, combine the Straub Beer, oil, garlic, salt, and pepper. Pour the mixture over the beef. Cover and refrigerate the beef, turning occasionally, for 1 hour. Sprinkle it with beef bouillon. In a casserole dish, place the beef fat side up on the rack. Reserve the marinade. Cook the roast at 325° for 1½ - 2 hours for medium doneness. Cover the roast with foil and let stand for 15 minutes. The roast will continue to cook. For the gravy, pour the drippings into a bowl and skim off the fat. Add the reserved marinade and enough water to make 1 cup. Shake the water and flour in a covered container and stir into the gravy. Enjoy!

This Straub Beer Garlic Roast Beef recipe from *The Straub Beer Cookbook* was served at the 2004 Straub Beer Food Fest. (Courtesy of Stohn Books.)

Fr. Paul Taylor has often said mass in honor of the Straub family and brewery before celebrations such as family reunions. (Photograph by Barbara Schlimm.)

Before dinner, there are always fun games to be played in Straub Country. Here, many of the younger Straub cousins play a game under the old apple tree in Straub Bear Run in 2000. (Photograph by Barbara Schlimm.)

Straub

SINCE 1872

BEER & LIGHT

Write from the kettle...

Straub Beer Sunrise

12 ounces Straub Beer
1 ounce amaretto
1 ounce orange juice
Orange slice

Combine all of the ingredients on the rocks, stirring well. Garnish with the orange slice.

Straub Brewery, Inc. • 303 Sorg Street • St. Marys, PA 15857
(814) 834-2875 • Fax (814) 834-7628 • www.straubbeer.com

This drink recipe from *The Straub Beer Party Drinks Handbook* was served along with other Straub beer drink selections at the 2004 Straub Beer Food Fest. (Courtesy of Stohn Books.)

Parties in Straub Country are never limited to just people. Here, Peter's great-grandson Jack Schlimm welcomes a few waddling guests to a party in the 1970s. (Photograph by Allen Herr.)

Peter's great-grandson-in-law Joe Koch is one of Straub Country's favorite cooks. For many years, he catered the meals for family reunions and other brewery parties, leaving each guest with an authentic taste of Straub hospitality. (Courtesy of Straub Brewery.)

Straub
SINCE 1872
BEER & LIGHT

Write from the kettle...

Straub Beer Salsa

6 chile peppers, 1 cup Straub Beer, 1 clove garlic, juice from 1 orange, 1/4 medium onion (chopped), Salt (to taste), 1/2 cup white cheese (crumbled), and tortilla chips

In a skillet, toast the chiles over a medium heat/flame until they blister. Open the chiles and remove the stems, veins, and seeds. Soak the chiles in the Straub Beer for 30 minutes. In a blender, combine the chiles, Straub Beer, garlic, and orange juice, pureeing until the mixture is smooth. Stir in the onion and add the salt. Garnish with the cheese and serve.

Straub Brewery, Inc. • 303 Sorg Street • St. Marys, PA 15857
(814) 834-2875 • Fax (814) 834-7628 • www.straubbeer.com

This is a recipe for Straub Beer Salsa. (Courtesy of JES II.)

The buffets in Straub Country, such as this one for a brewery picnic in the 1970s, always leave guests full and satisfied. (Courtesy of Straub Brewery.)

Here, Carl and Ann Straub are enjoying their dinner at a brewery picnic in the 1960s. Carl worked in the office at the brewery for many years. (Courtesy of Straub Brewery.)

Write from the kettle...

*Straub Beer
Dried Tomato Bread*

1/4 cup sugar, 3 1/2 cups self-rising flour, 12 ounces Straub Beer, 1 egg, 1/4 cup tomato sauce, and 2 ounces dried tomatoes

Preheat the oven to 350°. In a medium bowl, combine the sugar and flour, mixing well. Add the Straub Beer, egg, and tomato sauce, mixing well. Fold in the dried tomatoes. Place the dough into a greased loaf pan. Bake the dough for approximately 1 hour. Cool the loaf on a wire rack.

Straub Brewery, Inc. • 303 Sorg Street • St. Marys, PA 15857
(814) 834-2875 • Fax (814) 834-7628 • www.straubbeer.com

This is a recipe for Straub Beer Dried Tomato Bread. (Courtesy of JES II.)

Music and singing are always a part of any party in Straub Country, such as at this brewery picnic in the 1980s. Charles Stanish on accordion is surrounded by, from left to right, Peter's granddaughter Betty Bosnik, Reggie Straub, Laura Straub, Toots Nero, Kathleen Simbeck, and Irma Skok.

In addition to leading the songs during the Straub family's Fourth of July parade, here Blondie Straub Taylor is leading an after-dinner rendition of the traditional German folk song "Schnitzelbank" at a Straub family reunion. (Photograph by Barbara Schlimm.)

Straub

SINCE 1872
BEER & LIGHT

Write from the kettle...

Straub Beer Sweet & Sour Trout   Serves 6-8

1/4 cup butter, 2 onions (chopped), 2 tablespoons all-purpose flour, 12 ounces Straub Beer, 2 tablespoons brown sugar, 5 peppercorns, 2 cloves, 1 teaspoon Worcestershire sauce, 3 pounds trout fillets (cut into bite-size pieces), and 1 tablespoon vinegar

In a skillet, combine the butter and onions, sautéing the onions until they are tender. Add the flour and cook for 3 minutes. Add the Straub Beer, brown sugar, peppercorns, cloves, and Worcestershire sauce, cooking over a low heat and stirring until the mixture is thickened. Add the trout and cook, covered, until the fillets are done. Add the vinegar and cook for 2 more minutes.

Straub Brewery, Inc. • 303 Sorg Street • St. Marys, PA 15857
(814) 834-2875 • Fax (814) 834-7628 • www.straubbeer.com

This is a recipe for Straub Beer Sweet and Sour Trout. (Courtesy of JES II.)

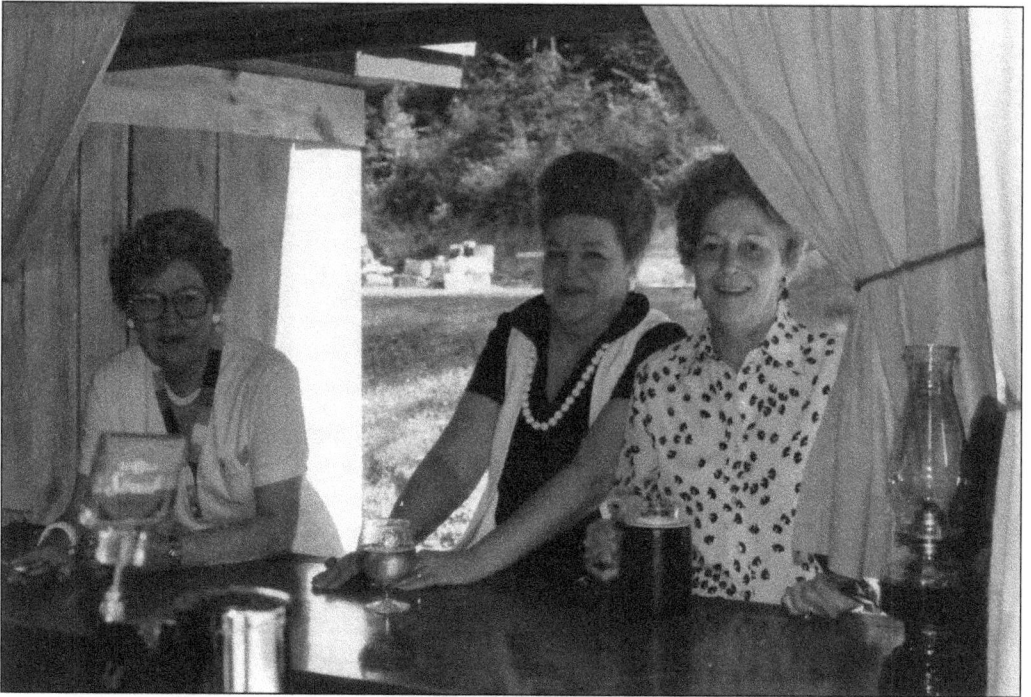

Here, Peg Straub, Mary Straub, and Laura Straub, all over 21 and not driving, enjoy "one for the road" in Straub Country. (Courtesy of JES II.)

Laughter is always at the top of the menu for any celebration in Straub Country. That classic humor is evident in the words gracing this outhouse at Uncle Pete's Camp. Indeed, this is the site of the *other* Eternal Tap. (Photograph by Allen Herr.)

126

Straub
SINCE 1872
BEER & LIGHT

Write from the kettle...

Straub Beer
Chocolate-Dipped Bananas

Serves 4

4 bananas (firm, peeled, and cut into 3 pieces), 2 cups Straub Beer batter (2 cups flour + 1 pint Straub Beer blended until smooth), oil, juice from 2 lemons, 1/2 cup honey, 1 cup whipped cream (add a little sugar to enhance flavoring), and chocolate (melted)

Coat the bananas with the Straub Beer batter. In a skillet, heat the oil to 350°. Add the bananas, cooking them until they are golden and crispy. Remove the bananas and sprinkle them with the lemon juice and honey. Top the bananas with the sweetened whipped cream and serve them with the dipping chocolate.

Straub Brewery, Inc. • 303 Sorg Street • St. Marys, PA 15857
(814) 834-2875 • Fax (814) 834-7628 • www.straubbeer.com

This is a recipe for Straub Beer Chocolate-Dipped Bananas. (Courtesy of JES II.)

"I hope this journal finds you well, happy, and full of good beer!" —Mary Fox Sinclair Huffman (Peter Straub's great-granddaughter), Straub Family Time Capsule journal, July 1, 2000. (Photograph by Jim Straub, courtesy of Jack Schlimm.)

www.ingramcontent.com/pod-product-compliance
Lightning Source LLC
Chambersburg PA
CBHW050558110426
42813CB00008B/2397